The Violent

Are Taking It

By Force

Aggressively Taking What Belongs to You in the Name of JESUS

Dr Michael H Yeager

(Some of the teaching in this book is taken from the Adam Clarke Commentary, and other non-copyright material found on the internet)

ISBN:1481219308
ISBN-13:9781481219303

DEDICATION

All of the Scriptures used in this book: **"The Violent Are Taking It By Force"** are taken from the original 1611 version of the King James Bible. I give thanks to God the Father, Jesus Christ and the Holy Ghost for the powerful impact the Word has had upon my life. Without the Word Quickened in my heart by the Holy Ghost, I would have been lost and undone. I am eternally indebted to the Lord of Heaven and Earth, for His great love and His mercy, His protections and His provisions, His divine guidance and overwhelming goodness. The Price He PAID for my Healing! To Him be glory and praise for ever and ever: Amen

WE CANNOT BE DEFEATED WHEN WE ARE WALKING & MOVING WITH A FAITH THAT WILL NOT TAKE NO FOR AN ANSWER!

To Obtain the Kingdom of God, its blessings and provisions, you need to rise up with a Radical, Violent, Aggressive, Faith. The author has apprehended many of God's blessings because he Took by Violent Faith what God had promised him. He would not let go of God's Promises until he had obtained the Promised Blessing. This book is filled with radical stories of the author, and others, who knew the will of God and did not care if they lived or died, to obtain what God said He Had Given to them. Remember, God is not a respecter of persons. What HE has done for others HE will do for YOU!

Dr Michael H Yeager

CONTENTS

ACKNOWLEDGMENTS

*To our Heavenly Father and His wonderful love.

*To our Lord, Savior and Master — Jesus Christ, who saved us and set us free because of His great love for us.

*To the Holy Spirit, who leads and guides us into the realm of truth and miraculous living every day.

*To all of those who had a part in helping me get this book ready for the publishers.

*To my Lovely Wife Kathleen, and our precious children: Michael, Daniel, Steven, Stephanie, our precious daughter-in-law Catherine Yu, and Naomi, who is now with the Lord.

Important Introduction!

The experiences of **VIOLENT FAITH** that I have personally witnessed and shared in this book are all true. These experiences have either happened to me, my family or others.

By no means do the following stories account for all of the Provisions and Miracles that I have seen, and experienced, in my life. If I were to recount every single answer, to every single prayer, and every wonderful healing, miracle and blessing - there would be no end to this book!

What I share with you in this book are simply highlights of what I have experienced in the Lord. Some of these experiences will seem incredulous. However, they are all true! This is not a testimony of how spiritual I am, or how spiritual we are, but of how wonderful and marvelous the Father, the Son, and the Holy Ghost are.

I share these experiences to the best of my recollections and understanding. Not every conversation is exactly word for word; I would love to name every person that was a part of these wonderful occurrences, but privacy laws do not allow this. If you are reading this book and you either saw, experienced, or were a part of these events, please do not be offended because your names are not mentioned.

The Violent Are Taking It By Force

CHAPTER ONE

The Violent Take It By FORCE! (2013)

Back in 2013 I was lying in bed when I heard the **audible voice of God. HE** said to me: **"The violent take it by force!"** For a while now this has been marinating in my soul. Sometimes when God speaks to me it takes time for it to become a reality. It could be four years later, or maybe even decades later, as the spirit of God is at work on my insides. You could say it is rather like a pregnant woman: life is growing inside of her womb. Instead of saying: 'the violent take it by force' you could say: **'The Violent Take It by Faith!'** Even so, **FAITH** begins as a seed, and must grow within us, in our hearts. We have a lot to do with that faith growing, expanding, enlarging and becoming mature.

Please understand, everybody has **Faith**. Everyone was born with a measure, a proportion of **Faith.** When Jesus shared the parable of the ten virgins who were asleep, He said they all woke up when the trumpet sounded; but there were five foolish virgins and five wise virgins. It was only the five wise virgins that had enough oil to take them to the arrival of their Husband to be. I believe that one of the realities of the oil Jesus was speaking of is the **oil of Faith**. I believe it is faith in God and faith in Jesus Christ.

People who do not have sufficient **FAITH,** in this time period, are going to have it rough. They are going to try to find somebody that does have faith, but it will be too late. Then there are those who do have faith, but it has been in hibernation.

Faith can be lying dormant inside of you for many years. Then suddenly something supernatural happens, and it begins to come forth; like a bear coming out of hibernation!

Hebrews 11:32-34 And what shall I more say? for the time would fail me to tell of Gedeon, and of Barak, and of Samson, and of Jephthae; of David also, and Samuel, and of the prophets: 33 Who through faith subdued kingdoms, wrought righteousness, obtained promises, stopped the mouths of lions, 34 Quenched the violence of fire, escaped the edge of the sword, out of weakness were made strong, waxed valiant in fight, turned to flight the armies of the aliens.

#1 GOD Said: You Better Not Lie or You'll Die!

One day (1981) I picked up a book by a well-known author. The book was highly recommended by one of my favorite preachers at that time; the topic was angelic visitations. This was something I was interested in because of my many experiences with the supernatural. I began to read the book, and noticed immediately there were experiences he said he'd had, which did not seem to line up with the Scriptures. I did not want to judge his heart, but we do have the responsibility to examine everything in light of God's Word. If it does not line up with the Word of God then we must reject it - no matter who wrote it.

As I was pondering the stories in the book, the Spirit of the Lord spoke to my heart very strongly. It was as if He was standing right there next to me, speaking audibly. What He said to me was rather shocking! The Lord told me that the writer of the book would be dead in three months from a heart attack! I asked the Lord why He was telling me this; He said the stories in the man's book were exaggerated, and that judgment was coming. The Lord warned me that day that if I were ever to do the same thing, judgment would come to me too. I did not realize, back then, that the Lord would later have me writing books - many of them filled with my own personal experiences. Now I know why He spoke this to me, telling me that I better not exaggerate my experiences!

When the Spirit of the Lord spoke to me, I turned and told my wife. I held the book up and in a very quiet, whispering, trembling, wavering voice, I said: "Honey, the man who wrote this book will be dead in three months from a heart attack!" I went on to explain to her why the Lord had told me this. I wish I had been wrong. Exactly three months later the man died from a heart attack. God can speak to us through the positive and the negative circumstances of life. We better take heed to what He is saying!

How to Possess Aggressive, Radical, Violent Faith

Before we go any further in this teaching, you have the right to ask: "What authority do you have to write such a book as this?" Let me answer this question with a look at The Apostle Paul. The Corinthian church had been invaded by teachers who had a big talk, but they had no walk to back it up. It's amazing how people who have no experience, try to inform those who do have experience, what to do. How did Paul deal with all of the people who presented themselves as experts? Well … he shared his experiences!

2 Corinthians 11:22-28 Are they Hebrews? so am I. Are they Israelites? so am I. Are they the seed of Abraham? so am I. 23 Are they ministers of Christ? (I speak as a fool) I am more; in labours more abundant, in stripes above measure, in prisons more frequent, in deaths oft. 24 Of the Jews five times received I forty stripes save one. 25 Thrice was I beaten with rods, once was I stoned, thrice I suffered shipwreck, a night and a day I have been in the deep; 26 In journeyings often, in perils of waters, in perils of robbers, in perils by mine own countrymen, in perils by the heathen, in perils in the city, in perils in the wilderness, in perils in the sea, in perils among false brethren; 27 In weariness and painfulness, in watchings often, in hunger and thirst, in fastings often, in cold and nakedness. 28 Beside those things that are without, that which cometh upon me daily, the care of all the churches.

Please notice that his credentials were the trials and the tests God had brought him through. When I listen to teachers and preachers of the Word of God I am always looking for evidence of their own experiences, in their own lives.

Revelation 12:11 And they overcame him by the blood of the Lamb, and by the word of their testimony; and they loved not their lives unto the death.

PASTOR MIKE: WHY DO YOU GET ATTACKED SO MUCH BY THE DEVIL? You see, I have been HEALED of at least **Twenty** major ailments! Without the use of medicine or doctors!!

#1   Healed of major allergies
#2   Healed of loss of the sense of smell
#3   Healed of birth defects in the bones of my ears
#4   Healed of a speech impediment
#5   Healed of a broken back

#6 Healed of burned out vocal cords
#7 I was raised from the dead by my wife
#8 Healed of painful tumors in my abdomen
#9 Healed of a serious hernia
#10 Healed of a broken and crushed kneecap
#11 Healed of a dangerous attack of conjunctivitis
#12 Healed of arthritis
#13 Healed instantly of a broken foot
#14 My son was Healed from rabies
#15 Healed from prostate cancer
#16 Healed from life-threatening colon cancer
#17 Healed instantly of a broken, twisted index finger
#18 Healed overnight of second-degree burns
#19 Healed of gushing bright red blood
#20 And many Healings, on a daily basis since February 18, 1975.

PLEASE UNDERSTAND I AM BRAGGING ON JESUS!

I have experienced the enemy trying to Kill Me - and my loved ones - over **Fifty** times! In all of those dangerous situations (many times it looked like I was a goner!) God miraculously stepped in and delivered me. You might ask: **But How Pastor Mike?** and I would tell you that it was a **Violent FAITH in Christ** that preserved me.

*In the natural I should have been dead when the gang leader tried to stab me to death.
*When the same man shot me with a 12-gauge shotgun.
*I should have been dead when the Yupik Indians tried to steam me to death.
*I should have been dead when I fell into the Bering sea in rough weather.
*I should have been dead when my motorcycle flipped out underneath me, on black ice, on the main Highway.

5

*I should have been dead when the demon-possessed woman kept stabbing me in the face with a knife.

I COULD TELL YOU STORY AFTER STORY!
(Over 400 to date)

I asked the Lord: "Father, why in the world have I gone through so much?" He spoke to my heart and said: "I Will Use You As an Example Of What I Can Do in a Person's Life - If They Will Have **Faith in Me!**" But, I said Lord: "Why Me?" And He answered: "I Use the Foolish To Confound the Wise!"

1 Corinthians 1:27 But God hath chosen the foolish things of the world to confound the wise; and God hath chosen the weak things of the world to confound the things which are mighty;

Do Not Think for a Moment that I am bragging on Mike Yeager. I actually wrote a book called: **"I Need God Because I'm Stupid."**

That particular book was written for the total purpose of causing people to realize that Mike Yeager is nobody. It is Jesus Christ that we put our complete confidence and hope in. If God can use Mike Yeager: I can guarantee that He can use anybody! It is our faith in Christ that gives us the victory.

1 John 5:4-5 For whatsoever is born of God overcometh the world: and this is the victory that overcometh the world, even our faith. 5 Who is he that overcometh the world, but he that believeth that Jesus is the Son of God?

The testing and trying of our **Faith** are simply **Opportunities to Trust God**! These are testimonies of **Gods Power**! Of course, many times I have opened the door to the enemy by not using wisdom. But God has always been there to restore me. Believe me, these healings, deliverances, and miracles did not come easy! I could have taken the pathway of least resistance by running to the medical world for my healing. In my heart of hearts, I knew, that I knew, that I knew, by the **Stripes of Jesus Christ I am Healed**! I also knew that Jesus was my only hope in many dire circumstances. I Pray with All My Heart That As You Continue to Read This Book **FAITH** will come exploding into your inner being. And that faith in Christ will bring you into a place Of Amazing Victory!

EXAMPLE OF THE GIFT OF FAITH IN OPERATION!

#2 My Broken Foot Instantly Healed!

One day I had to climb our 250-foot AM radio tower in order to change the lightbulb on the main beacon. However, to climb the tower I had to first find the keys - which I never did. Since I could not find the keys to get the fence open, I did the next best thing: I simply climbed over the fence.

This turned out not to be such a wonderful idea after all! With all of my climbing gear hanging from my waist, I climbed the fence to the very top. At this point, my rope gear became entangled in the fencing. As I tried to get free, I lost my balance and fell backwards off the fence. Trying to break my fall, I got my right foot down underneath me; I hit the ground with my foot being turned on its side and felt something snap in my ankle. I knew instantly I had a broken foot, my ankle.

Most normal people would have climbed back over the fence, set up a doctor's appointment, had their foot x-rayed, and placed into a cast. But ... I am not a normal-thinking person. At least according to the standards of the modern day church. When I broke my foot, I followed my regular routine of confessing my **stupidity** to God and asked Him to forgive me for my stupidity.

Moreover, **I then Spoke To My Foot** and commanded it to be healed in the name of **Jesus Christ of Nazareth**! When I had finished speaking to my foot - commanding it to be healed - I began praising and thanking God for the healing. At that moment there was no change whatsoever with the condition of my foot.

The Scripture that came to my heart was when **Jesus** declared:
Matthew 11:12: "...The kingdom of heaven suffereth violence, and the violent take it by force!" Based completely upon this Scripture, I decided that I needed to exercise my faith: by climbing the 250-foot tower. With my broken foot. Please do not misunderstand, my foot hurt so bad I could not really stand on it. I had declared that I believed I was healed, so in my heart I had to act upon this truth.

James 1:22 But be ye doers of the word, and not hearers only, deceiving your own selves.

There were three men watching me as I took the **Word of God by faith**. I told them what I was about to do, and they looked at me like I had lost my mind. I began to climb the **250-foot tower, one painful step at a time**. My foot hurt so bad that I was hyperventilating within just twenty to thirty feet up the tower. It felt like I was going to pass out from shock at any moment. Whenever I got close to the point of **fainting**, I would connect my climbing ropes to the tower, stop, take a breather and cry out to Jesus to help me. It seemed to take forever to get to the top.

Even so, I finally reached the very top of the tower and replaced the lightbulb. Usually, I can get down that tower in ten minutes. I would press my feet against the tower rods, and then slide down - just using my hands and arms to lower myself at a very fast pace. However, in this situation, my foot could not handle the pressure of being pushed up against the steel. Consequently, I had to work my way down - very slowly.

What would normally take me around half-an-hour, ended up taking over one-hour. It was a long, painful and terrible trial. After I was down, I slowly climbed over the fence one more time. I dragged myself over to my vehicle, slowly got into it, and drove up to the church office. The men who had been watching this unfold were right behind me.

I hobbled my way into the front office of the church that I pastored, and informed my office personnel that I had broken my foot. I showed them **my black and blue, extremely swollen, big-time broken foot** and told them that I was going home to rest. At the same time, however, I told them that I believed, according to God's Word, that I was healed.

Going home, which is directly across from the main office of the church parking lot, I slowly made my way up the stairs to our bedroom. I found my wife in our bedroom putting away our clothes. Slowly and painfully I pulled the shoe and sock off of the broken foot.

What a mess! It was fat, swollen, black and blue all over. I put a pillow down at the end of the bed and carefully pulled myself up onto the bed. Lying on my back, I tenderly placed my broken, swollen foot onto the pillow. No matter how I positioned it, the pain did not cease. I just laid there squirming, moaning and sighing.

As I was lying there, trying to overcome the shock that kept hitting my body, I heard the **Audible voice of God**. He said to me: **"What are you doing in bed?"** God really got my attention when I heard Him with my natural ears. My wife would testify that she heard nothing. Immediately in my heart I said: **"Lord, I'm just resting."** Then He spoke to my heart with the still, small, voice very clearly: "Do you always rest at this time of day?" I replied: "No, Lord" (It was about 3 o'clock in the afternoon).

He spoke to my heart again and He said: **"I thought you said you were healed?"** At that very moment the Gift of Faith exploded inside of me. I said: **"Lord, I am healed!"**

(When the gift of Faith is in operation, there is no maybe, if, or but: You Know, That You Know, That You Know, It Is Done!)

Immediately, I pushed myself up off the bed, grabbed my sock and shoe, and struggled to put them back on. What a tremendous struggle it was! My foot was so swollen that it did not want to go into the shoe. My wife was watching me as I fought to complete this task. You might wonder what my wife was doing this whole time, as I was fighting this battle of **FAITH** - she was doing what she always does - watching me and shaking her head. I finally got the shoe back on. I put my foot down on the floor and began to put my body weight upon it. When I did this, I almost passed out. At that moment, a **Holy Anger** exploded inside of me.

I declared out loud: **"I am healed in the name of Jesus Christ of Nazareth!"** With that declaration, I took my right (broken) foot, and slammed it down onto the floor as hard as I possibly could.

I felt the bones of my foot break even more. Like the Fourth of July, an explosion of blue, purple, red, white and black exploded in my brain and **I passed out**. I came to, lying on my bed. Afterwards, my wife informed me that every time I passed out, it was for about ten to twenty seconds. The moment I came to, **I jumped right back up out of bed**.

The gift of faith was working in me mightily. I got back up and followed the same process: **"In the name of Jesus Christ of Nazareth I am healed,"** and slammed my foot down once more as hard as I could! For a second time, I could feel the damage in my foot increasing. My mind was once again wrapped in an explosion of colors and pain as I blacked out.

When I regained consciousness, I immediately got up once again, repeating the same process. After the third time of this happening, I came to, with my wife leaning over the top of me. I remember my wife saying as she looked at me: "You are making me sick. I can't watch you do this." She promptly walked out of our bedroom and went downstairs.

The fourth time I got up declaring: **"In the name of Jesus Christ of Nazareth I am healed,"** and slammed my foot even harder! Once more, multiple colors of intense pain hit my brain. I passed out again! I got up the fifth time, angrier than ever. This was not a demonic or proud anger. **This was a divine gift of violent 'I-will-not-take-no-for-an-answer' type of FAITH.** I slammed my foot down the fifth time: **"In the name of Jesus Christ of Nazareth I am healed!"**

The minute my foot slammed onto the floor, for the fifth time, the power of God hit my foot. I stood under the quickening power of God and **watched my foot shrink - and become normal - in less than thirty seconds.** All of the pain was completely and totally gone.

I pulled back my sock, and watched the black and blue in my foot disappear to normal flesh color. I was healed! Praise God! I was made whole. I went back to the office, giving glory to the Lord the whole time, and showed the staff my healed foot.

As I have shared this story throughout the years, you cannot believe what some believers will say. One of them dogmatically declared that this could not be of God. His reasoning was that God would not require such an act of Faith. I guess he did not read about God requiring Abraham to put his son, Isaac, upon the altar. He did not read about God requiring His son, Jesus Christ, to take upon Himself the sins of the world; to be beaten with a cat-o-nine tails upon the whipping post; to be nailed to a tree, and to die for our sins.

There are many examples of God requiring His people to take radical steps of faith - in order that His will be done in the earth. If I had stopped at the fourth slamming of my foot to the floor, I definitely would have been in much worse shape than when I began. But thank God The Violent Gift of Faith was at work inside of me. I completed the divine task, and was rewarded with complete healing.

Many Believers Do Not Get HEALED Because They Are Spiritual Pacifists!

Numbers 23:19 God is not a man, that he should lie; neither the son of man, that he should repent: hath he said, and shall he not do it? or hath he spoken, and shall he not make it good?

When the enemy comes in like a flood, if I trust God, and act upon the Word: God will raise up a standard against the enemy. I'm amazed at how many modern believers are such pacifists when it comes to fighting off the enemy, by **Faith in Christ**. You have to rise up in the **Name of Jesus Christ** and speak against the circumstance that is contrary to God's will. If the circumstance does not seem to change, you do not let go of God's promises. You maintain a thankful and worshipful heart towards the Lord. Here is an illustration in my personal life.

Back in around 2009, I was lying in bed and all night long I'd had terrible pain racking my body. The whole time I was fighting the fight of **Faith**, speaking the Word, and praying quietly as I lay in my bed; I never allow a spirit of fear to control and dictate my actions.

The next thing I knew, my left hand went completely numb and all my fingers curled up. The devil said to me: "you're having a stroke." I Immediately jumped out of bed, took my numb left arm, with its curled up fingers, and began to **beat it against my right hand, commanding it to be healed**. I knew that this circumstance was not of God because by His stripes we are healed! I had to rise in the **Spirit Of Faith speaking** to this circumstance, in and by, the **Name of Jesus**.

With over forty years of practice, I know in most situations, what is, and what is not, the will of God. After I had commanded my arm, my hand and my body to be healed, I began to **Thank the Lord** that it was done. Now, in the natural my arm and my hand were still in the same condition as they were before I spoke to them in the **name of Jesus**, but I know that God Cannot Lie.

Praise the Lord that within a short period of time my left arm and hand were completely restored, and all the pain left my body! We should never give in to the lies, or the symptoms that the enemy is trying to use against us. The minute the enemy sticks his ugly head up we need to cut it off with the Word of God.

When I was a kid, we used to fish in a favorite fishing hole. It was filled with pan fish, crop-pies, and bluegills. The only problem was that it also had lots of mud turtles. These nasty turtles would kill anything that was in their path. Whenever we went fishing, we always carried our .22 Rifles: when these mud turtles stuck their heads up, we popped them with our rifles.

We were not going to allow them to devour the fish we were trying to catch. If we had not done this, there would have been no fish left in this pond! It is the same way spiritually: you cannot allow the devil and his demonic host to simply run over you. We must rise up, and overcome spiritual pacifism.

Matthew 16:19 And I will give unto thee the keys of the kingdom of heaven: and whatsoever thou shalt bind on earth shall be bound in heaven: and whatsoever thou shalt loose on earth shall be loosed in heaven.

UNDERSTANDING WHY YOU NEED VIOLENT FAITH

When Jesus said: *Matthew 11:11-12: "Verily I say unto you, Among them that are born of women there hath not risen a greater than John the Baptist: notwithstanding he that is least in the kingdom of heaven is greater than he. 12 <u>And from the days of John the Baptist until now the kingdom of heaven suffereth violence, and the violent take it by force.</u>"* What exactly was He referring to?

Throughout this book, by God's grace, I hope to reveal exactly what He meant. Let's begin by breaking down this statement, discovered in Matthew chapter 11, beginning with verse 11:

"Verily I say unto you, Among them that are born of women there hath not risen a greater than John the Baptist: notwithstanding he that is least in the kingdom of heaven is greater than he." Notice that in this amazing statement John the Baptist was considered the greatest! Yet, Jesus also said that the smallest, littlest, most humble member can operate in a realm that John the Baptist could only imagine. How could this be possible?

When Jesus was speaking to those who believed in Him, He declared in John 14:12: *"Verily, verily, I say unto you, He that believeth on me, the works that I do shall he do also; and greater works than these shall he do; because I go unto my Father."*

Notice what else Jesus boldly declared in Matthew 10:8: *"Heal the sick, cleanse the lepers, raise the dead, cast out devils: freely ye have received, freely give."*

The Apostle Paul gives us insight into how this works in the book of Galatians 3:5: *"He therefore that ministereth to you the Spirit, and worketh miracles among you, doeth he it by the works of the law, or by the hearing of faith?"*

Yes, it all comes back to having absolute and unwavering faith in God the Father, Jesus Christ, and the Word of God! Let us now take a look at the next verse:

Matthew 11:12 And from the days of John the Baptist until now the kingdom of heaven suffereth violence, and the violent take it by force. I like another translation that says: *"Men using force have been seizing it! Taken by storm, or by force. Violent are taking it: eager souls are storming it. Seizing it as a precious prize.*

*This Is Not A Violence Of Flesh Or Soul But Spirit!

Let us read verse 12 in this way: *"Those who are possessed of eagerness and zeal, instead of yielding to the opposition of life, press their way into the kingdom, so as to possess it for themselves."*

The Bible is filled with tremendous examples of this. For example, when God gave Canaan to the seed of Abraham; it was theirs, but they had to go in and take it from their enemy first. The first generation lost out because of unbelief. They could not, or let's say, would not, Trust, Believe, or Look to God for their victory over the enemy.

Not too long ago, I was in the sanctuary of the church I pastor. I was simply in prayer, crying out to God for His will to be done: in every area of my life, and in others' lives. As I was in prayer I heard the Lord, in my heart, say: **"Do You Know Why I Always Heal You?"**

Pastor Mike: How do you know this is God speaking to you?

16

Because over 90% of the time He always asks me questions about nothing that I am presently praying or thinking about. I know this is not a trick of my mind because I'm not even meditating upon what He says to me at the time. Plus, it does not contradict His Will, His Word, or His Personality.

I responded to the Lord with my own question. I said: "Lord, what do you mean?" He asked me again: "**Do You Know Why I Always Heal You?**" My mind was blank at this question so I said: "How Come, Lord?"

He said this to me: "**Because You Are Not Afraid to Die!**" The moment He said this, I knew that it was true. It is not that I want to die, because I know the Lord has so many more things that He still wants me to do. But I am not afraid to die **Believing His Word!**

As I stood there, on that day, my mind ran through many occasions when, in the natural, I should have gone to the arm of the flesh.

Something in my heart though wouldn't allow me to. It's what we call **Violent Faith**! It is not a thing of pride or arrogance. It's simply that, in my heart, for me to run to the world for my physical needs is literally to call God a liar.

For over forty years, I have simply stood upon God's Word. Even though, for months at times I have endured pain-filled days, all-night wrestling's with tears and groanings, yet I have stood upon God's Word. God, in every circumstance, has always brought to me Supernatural Deliverance!

The Violent Take HEALING

This statement may seem presumptuous or inaccurate, but believe me - it is the truth. It is built on the biblical principles of faith and obedience to the will of God.

Most Bible believing Christians will acknowledge that all that ever needed to be done, was accomplished when Christ went to the cross, died and rose again. The Scriptures declare we were healed by the stripes upon the back of Jesus.

This is not just pertaining to spiritual healing, but absolutely also implies physical healing. God took me to the Scriptures within the first month that I was saved (in 1975) pertaining to the subject of healing. There are many Scriptures that deal with this, but more specifically: Isaiah 53, Matthew 8:17, and first Peter 2:24. After I studied and meditated upon the Scriptures, faith rose in my heart, and I literally took the Word of God, aggressively, for my own healing. I was healed from lifelong illnesses and generational curses.

Yet, still today many believers - in spite of the Scriptures declaring that Jesus paid the ultimate price for our physical healing - are having a difficult time receiving their healing. There are reasons for this. I actually did a teaching entitled: "30 Reasons Why Christians Are Not Healed." That may sound like I have made it extremely complicated, but in truth it's not.

#3 HOW My Burned Out Vocal Cords Were Healed
(1979)

My wife and I were attending Rhema Bible Training Center. We had arrived in Oklahoma (with a Ford F250 four-wheel drive) but now that school was about finished, we had to make a choice. What would be the best vehicle for us to travel in? We determined that we should sell the truck, pay the bills and buy an old work van. The van that we bought needed much work: mechanical, exterior and interior. We covered the inside of the van with carpet and built a bed all the way in the back, so that when we were traveling we would not need to get a hotel. The day after graduation we had the van loaded, and were headed back to Pennsylvania.

There was only one major problem: the engine compartment was part-way on the inside of the van, and the valve covers were allowing oil to leak on top of the engine. This caused burning smoke to come inside the cabin. I determined that I could wait until I arrived in Pennsylvania to repair this problem.

Smoke started to fill the cabin: to the point where I had to roll down the driver and passenger windows - in order to breathe! My wife was okay because she stayed in the back of the van, lying on the bed. There was just no way that I could avoid the fumes. I breathed them in all the way from Broken Arrow, Oklahoma, to Mukwonago Wisconsin, to visit relatives. Then we traveled from Wisconsin to Mount Union, Pennsylvania. Over 1400 miles I drove that old van, breathing in those fumes. Close to twenty hours altogether!

You can imagine what kind of condition I was in by the time we arrived at our final destination. My lungs and my throat were burned raw. I was having a hard time breathing, and I could not speak. I naturally assumed that this would remedy itself within a few days. I could not have been more wrong! Being a preacher of the gospel, one of the most important tools at my disposal is my voice.

Ever since the Lord healed me of my speech impediment (I had been born tongue-tied) I was seldom ever quiet. I was always sharing Christ; preaching and sharing what Jesus had done for me. But now I could only speak, or preach, for probably less than ten minutes before my voice was gone. During this time, I would cry out to God, in a whisper, asking Him to help me and to restore my voice. This went on for what seemed to be months ... with very little results.

You see, I was making the same mistake that many people

make today: I did not need to ask God to heal me because He had already done it 2000 years ago! What I needed to do was take authority over this physical affliction and command it to go and my voice to be healed. I needed to command my vocal cords to be strong and healthy.

Beloved saints, we need to believe God to become impervious to destruction and damage. Impervious to destruction? What do I mean by that statement? Did not Jesus declare that He gave us power over the enemy? And that nothing shall by any means come to harm us? I am not suggesting that we tempt the Lord by doing foolish things. When we get into situations like this, we need to take the authority that we have in Jesus' name and take what belongs to us - because of what Christ accomplished for us.

After a while, I finally got fed up, disgusted, and angry with the throat and voice condition. I did not get angry with God, but with the devil, and with myself, for putting up with it.

You need to know who your enemy really is! Even if you're the one who opened the door for the enemy: you can repent of your stupidity and ask God to forgive you. Thereby, receiving forgiveness by faith. After you do this, it's time to go to war in order to take what is rightfully yours! Maybe some people would be curious as to why I did not run to the medical world? The truth of the matter is, I see sickness, disease and infirmity as a spiritual condition: if I deal with it in the spiritual, then it will be dealt with in the natural.

After one particular Sunday service, when I had once again lost my voice, I finally put my foot down … I went to the Father, in prayer, in the name of Jesus. I spoke to Him about all of the promises of healing and that being a child of God, healing is a part of the covenant He made with me. I knew that even in the old covenant, healing was available for God's people. I was not doing this because I thought the Lord needed to be reminded. I was doing it to build up my own faith - in light of the reality of my rights as a child of God. After a while I perceived in my heart that it was time to address the enemy about my throat and my vocal cords. I took the name of Jesus, speaking His Name in a whisper, and commanded my body to be healed and the works of the enemy to cease.

Once I had finished along this line, with a whisper, I began to praise God and worship His Name. Thanking Him that I was healed. No ifs, ands, or buts about it. I was healed! From that moment forward, no matter how I felt, I kept thanking God that I was healed.

This was not something I broadcast to anybody else. As far as I was concerned: I was healed! For the next couple of days I continually thanked the Lord, over and over, even though I could barely speak - just with a whisper. I was not trying to convince God, or myself, of this reality: I just knew, that I knew, that I knew that I was healed! A number of days went by, I woke up one morning with all of the symptoms gone. For the last thirty-seven years I have been able to preach like a house on fire! I very seldom (or never) lose my voice. It is the reality that "by His stripes we were healed" that gives us the victory!

We know that God cannot lie! If HE declared it, then it must be so!

CHAPTER TWO

OH! If Only God's People Would Take Him At His Word, He Would Have Delivered Them Speedily!

If you study the four gospels, you will discover that Jesus operated in violent faith! He was waging a battle against demonic powers and it took a bold, audacious, and determined faith to win over the enemy.

Acts 10:38 How God anointed Jesus of Nazareth with the Holy Ghost and with power: who went about doing good, and healing all that were oppressed of the devil; for God was with him.

1 John 3:8 He that committeth sin is of the devil; for the devil sinneth from the beginning. For this purpose the Son of God was manifested, that he might destroy the works of the devil.

*Jesus Said That The Strong And Forceful Ones Claim It For Themselves Eagerly.

Ephesians 6:10 Finally, my brethren, be strong in the Lord, and in the power of his might. **Be strong: manly vigor, firm, be determined, unwavering, none compromise.**

2 Samuel 22:40 For thou hast girded me with strength to battle: them that rose up against me hast thou subdued under me.

Philippians 4:13 I can do all things through Christ which strengtheneth me. Or: I am ready for anything through the strength of the one who lives within me.

Proverbs 24:10 If thou faint in the day of adversity, thy strength is small.

Now let us take a look at Luke 16. It is the same declaration, but with just a little bit of a different take:

Luke 16:15-17 And he said unto them, Ye are they which justify yourselves before men; but God knoweth your hearts: for that which is highly esteemed among men is abomination in the sight of God. 16 The law and the prophets were until John: since that time the kingdom of God is preached, and every man presseth into it. 17 And it is easier for heaven and earth to pass, than one tittle of the law to fail.

In Luke 16:16 everyone is storming, forcing his way into it.

*Please understand that the things of spirit do not come naturally. By faith, you have to fight your way into it.

Luke 13:24 Strive to enter in at the straight gate: for many, I say unto you, will seek to enter in and shall not be able. "Strain every nerve, fight your way, your utmost" *There Must be a striving, earnestness, determination, commitment, seriousness, aggressiveness, passion and resolution.

This Is A Good Description Of How Faith In Christ Operates.

"Natural" men see things only as they appear but "spiritual" men see things completely differently. There is a divine, inward violence called faith, that refuses to agree with the devil. It refuses to call God a liar by disagreeing with Him. **Violent Men of Faith** understand that **Change Will Not Come Without Confrontation**.

We have to confront ourselves, our circumstances and the demonic world: without compromising our character, attitude, or personality.

I love this quote from Smith Wigglesworth:

"This Is The Place Where God Will Show up! You must come to a place of ashes, a place of helplessness, a place of wholehearted surrender where you do not refer to yourself. You have no justification of your own in regard to anything. You are prepared to be slandered, to be despised by everybody. But because of His personality in you, He reserves you for Himself because you are godly, and He sets you on high because you have known His name (Ps. 91:14). He causes you to be the fruit of His loins and to bring forth His glory so that you will no longer rest in yourself. Your confidence will be in God. Ah, it is lovely. 'The Lord is the Spirit; and where the Spirit of the Lord is, there is liberty' (2 Cor. 3:17)."

Violent faith always runs towards the enemy - not away from. David, the young Shepherd boy, is a perfect example of this when he ran towards Goliath. Not only did he boldly declare to the men of Israel, King Saul, and others, that he was not afraid of this uncircumcised Philistine; but he would willingly challenge him. He did not boast, or brag about himself, he exalted God! He told them that the same God that delivered the lion and the bear into his hands, would also deliver this uncircumcised Philistine into his hands. **Violent Faith never exhorts the enemy, negative circumstances, sicknesses or diseases: It Exalts God!** Woe to the devil, if we, as God's people, ever get serious with God.

To fully understand what Jesus is saying in Luke 16, we must read the whole chapter. The chapter is a declaration of Violent Faith. It is dealing with the heart, and the nature, of one pursuing the will of God. From Luke chapter **16:1-8** it is talking about a worldly steward, who was determined to get the blessing. In verse **13** He tells us that you cannot please two masters. In verse **14** it tells us the Pharisees, who were covetous, mocked Jesus at the sayings. That is when Jesus declares that those who are operating by faith possess the kingdom. In verse **17** He shows us the foundation of this attitude. He says that heaven and earth will pass away, but God's Word means what it says, and says what it means!

Hebrews 6:18 That by two immutable things, in which it was impossible for God to lie, we might have a strong consolation, who have fled for refuge to lay hold upon the hope set before us:

Luke **18:1-8** is another amazing example of violent faith. Jesus shares with us about a widow woman who would not back off. Violent faith does not mean that you are ugly, nasty, mean, accusative or unforgiving. No. It is the opposite. Violent faith works by love for God - and others.

In Luke **18:2** the worldly judge cared for nothing. He was ungodly, heathenistic and an ignoramus of a judge. Yet, this did not stop the little widow lady - who was full of faith - from giving up! In Luke **18:3** this little lady knew that she had the right to Justice and Protection. ***If we are going to operate in Violent Faith, we will not take "No" for an answer. We Must know what is right!** However, it is not good enough just to 'know' what is right: "Yeah ... But God promised ..." No! Not good enough! You must be willing to fight by faith. In Luke **18:4** The unjust judge would not, for a while, listen to the widow! Notice in Luke **18:5** the use of the word "Yet"- because she keeps troubling him. The word 'trouble' means to annoy, be a nuisance and she wearies him with her persistence. Like a battering ram! She wears him thin.

We discover three elements in this type of **Faith: a) Determined b) Persistent c) Patient.** I'm sorry to say that these elements are mostly missing from modern day American Christianity. Most American Christians are swallowed up with the **Wimp factor**. They have become Quitters. They easily Give up. They have become a bunch of crybabies, thumb suckers, fault finders, and diaper-fillers.

*The widow had plenty of opportunities to make excuses and quit. But if, like the widow, you believe, trust and fight: God can and will turn any situation around. Passivity will kill you.

Isaiah 40:29 He giveth power to the faint; and to them that have no might he increaseth strength.

#4 My Broken Back Healed (1977)

I share these stories of my personal experiences hoping that they will give you an insight in how to receive healing, even in the most difficult situations. In the winter of 1977, I was working at the Belleville Feed & Grain Mill. My job was to pick up the corn, wheat, and oats from the farmers and take them to the mill. There they would be mixed and combined with other products for the farmers' livestock.

One cold and snowy day, the owner of the feed mill told me to deliver a load of cattle feed to an Amish farm. It was an extremely bad winter that year, with lots of snow. I was driving an International 1600 Lodestar. I backed up as far as I could to the Amish man's barn, without getting stuck. The Amish never had their lanes plowed in those days (and they most likely still don't) I was approximately seventy-five feet away from the barn, which meant that I had to carry the bags at least seventy-five feet. I think there were about eighty bags of feed: each bag weighing approximately 100 pounds. During those years I only weighed about 130 pounds myself.

I carried one bag on each shoulder, stumbling and pushing my way through the heavy and deep snow to get up the steep incline into the barn. Then I would stack the bags in a dry location. As usual, nobody came out to help me. Many a time, when delivering things to the farms, the Amish would watch me work without lending a helping hand. About the third trip, something frightening happened to me: I was carrying two 100 pound bags upon my shoulders when I felt the bones in my back snap. Something drastic had just happened! I fell to the ground at that very moment - almost completely crippled. I could barely move and I was filled with intense and overwhelming pain.

I had been spending a lot of my time meditating on the Word of God. Every morning I would get up about 5:00 a.m. to study. I had one of those little bread baskets with memorization scriptures in it. I believe you can still buy them to this day, at Christian bookstores. Every morning I'd memorize three to five of them. It did not take me very long and all day I would meditate on the verses.

The very minute I fell down, I immediately cried out to Jesus. I asked Him to forgive me for my pride, and for being so stupid in carrying two 100 pound bags on my little frame. After I asked Jesus to forgive me, I commanded my back to be healed in the name of Jesus Christ of Nazareth. Since I believed I was healed, I knew that **I had to act now upon my faith**. Please understand, I was full of tremendous pain, but I had declared that I was healed by the stripes of Jesus. The Word of God came out of my mouth as I tried to get up and then fell back down.

Even though the pain was more intense than I can express, I kept getting back up, speaking the name of Jesus; then I would fall back down again. I fell down more times than I can remember. After some time, I was able to take a couple of steps, then I would fall again. The entire time I was saying, **"In the name of Jesus, in the name of Jesus, in the name of Jesus."** I finally was able to get to the truck. I said to myself: "If I believe I'm healed, then I will unload this truck in the name of Jesus." Of course, I did not have a cell phone in order to call for help. And the Amish did not own any phones on their property. Now, even if they'd had a phone, I would not have called for help. I had already called upon my help! His name is Jesus Christ. I knew, in my heart, that by the stripes of Jesus I was healed. So, I pulled a bag off the back of the truck and let it fall on top of me. I would drag it a couple of feet, and then fall down.

Tears were running down my face as I spoke the Word of God over and over. By the time I was done, with all of the bags, the sun had already gone down. Maybe six or seven hours had gone by. I painstakingly pulled myself up into that big old 1600 Lodestar. It took everything within me to shift gears, push in the clutch, and drive it. I had to sit straight like a board all the way.

I finally got back to the feed mill late in the evening. Everybody had left for home - a long time ago - and the building was locked up. I struggled out of the Lodestar and stumbled and staggered over to my Ford pickup. I got into my pickup, and made it back to the converted chicken house. I went back to my cold, unheated, plywood-floor room, and it took everything in me to get my clothes off. It was a very rough and long night.

The next morning when I woke up, my body was so stiff that I could not bend in the least. I was like a board. Of course, I was not going to miss work - because by the stripes of Jesus I was healed. In order to get out of bed I had to literally roll off the bed, hitting the floor. Once I had hit the floor, it took everything for me to push myself back up into a sitting position. The tears were rolling down my face as I put my clothes and shoes on, which in itself was a miracle. I did get to work on time, though every step was excruciatingly painful. Remember, I was only twenty-one years old at the time, but I knew what **Faith** was and I knew what it wasn't. I knew that I was healed no matter how it looked: that by the stripes of Jesus Christ I was healed.

When I got to work I did not tell my boss that I had been seriously hurt the day before. I walked into the office and tried to hide the pain on my face. For some reason, he did not ask me what time I made it back to work. I did not tell him to change the time clock for me in order to be paid for all of the hours I was out on the job. They had me checked out at the normal quitting time. (The love of money is what causes a lot of people not to get healed.) My boss gave me an order for feed that needed to be delivered to a local farmer. If you have ever been to a feed and grain mill, you know that there is a large shoot where the feed comes out. After it has been mixed, you have to take your feed bag, and hold it up until it is filled. It creates tremendous strain on your arms and your back - even if you are healthy.

As I was filling the bag, it almost felt like I was going to pass out, because I was in immense pain. I simply said: "In the name of Jesus, in the name of Jesus, in the name of Jesus" under my breath. The second bag was even more difficult than the first bag, but I kept on saying, "In the name of Jesus." I began on the third bag, and as I was speaking the name of Jesus, the power of God hit my back and I was instantly, completely and totally healed from the top of my head to the tips of my toes. I was healed as I went on my way! My place of employment never did know what happened to me. That was thirty-eight years ago and my back is still healed by the stripes of Christ - to this day!

#5 I Took My Healing Today (May 5, 2017)

What I am about to tell you will sound extremely strange if you do not understand how **faith: talks, walks and reacts** to the circumstances of life. You cannot fake faith. Nor just confess it into existence. Faith is when you know, that you know, that you know, that you know, God's Word is true: and He cannot lie. It is when what God has said is more real to you than what your body tells you: circumstances, symptoms, or the experts of this world.

On the morning of May 5, 2017, my sons and daughter-in-law went with me to collect a load of firewood someone gave us. In the process of loading approximately a cord-and a-half of firewood my right foot began to hurt real bad. That's the same foot that I slammed down in about 1996 when it was broken. (The fifth time I slammed my foot down, it was instantly healed: I did this underneath the unction of the gift of faith.)

So, we were loading the firewood and my foot began to really hurt. I did not say a word to my sons or my daughter-in-law. I continued to work. Under my breath, I told the devil that he was a liar and I told my foot that it was healed. The symptoms did not dissipate or leave me - in the least. After we loaded the firewood, we ate at a Chinese restaurant before going home. Now, while the boys got busy unloading this firewood, I walked across the parking lot of our church, to my office, which is approximately 400 feet away. My foot was hurting so bad by this time that it was hard to put any weight on it whatsoever.

I got into my office and began to do some office work. I needed to go all the way to the front of our facility, to get a room ready for a guest speaker. The room is approximately 150 feet away from where my office is. As I went, my foot seemed to be getting worse. Of course, the devil, he's yakking away at me ... but I'm simply ignoring him.

I was done with the preparations and walked out of the room, and OH man - was my foot hurting! The spirit of faith rose up in me at that moment, and I slammed my right foot down - real hard. I said: "Devil, You're a Liar, and my foot is healed." I took about twenty-more-steps and it got worse. Once again, I said: "Devil You're a Liar, and my foot is healed." I slammed my right foot down again - real hard. I took about another ten-steps, and the devil told me that I have a major problem and that I won't be able to get rid of this foot problem so quick and easy.

In my heart, I laughed at the devil, because I have been through so much worse than this. The third time I slammed my foot down, speaking to the devil, and to my foot: "Devil in the Name of Jesus You're a Liar, and my foot is healed." I went on my way, rejoicing and ignoring the pain. I did not try to step lightly, but I made myself walk normally.

By the time I went the one-hundred feet (or more) to my office, the pain was completely gone. I was healed! Let me say that the manifestation of my healing was evident in my foot. I am not bragging about Mike Yeager. I am bragging about Jesus Christ and the Word of God! God cannot lie!

Pastor Mike: What if the manifestation had not happened so soon? My answer to that is: "**SO WHAT!**" Yes! "**So What!**" Let God be true, and everything else a lie. If you are not walking in this area, this realm, simply begin to give yourself to the Word of God in prayer and meditation - until it explodes in your heart. Until the Reality of the Truth overwhelms the lie.

The Lord spoke to my heart one Sunday morning, when I was in prayer and getting ready for church. He said to me: "Is the darkness greater than the light?" I said: "No Lord!" The Lord said: "**The Darkness Has No Power over the Light!**" The minute you step into the light the darkness must flee! It Has No Choice!

This is how the Kingdom of God works! **Whatever is born of God, overcomes the world by faith in Christ**. All I can say is: Thank You, Jesus!

The Danger of Being a Presumptuous Christian!

A number of years ago, a precious sister from my church walked past a group of men that were working on a pickup truck. Their car would not start. I do not believe the Holy Spirit told her to do this, she simply did it on her own.

She walked up to the men, working on the pickup truck, and asked: "what's wrong?" They looked at her like she had lost her mind. But, she felt bold in the Lord, so she asked again: "what's wrong?" They basically said: "DA--- the truck won't start." She said: "don't worry, I'll lay hands on this truck in the name of Jesus, and it will start!" Sounds wonderful - doesn't it? But, it was not God.

They looked at her again, like she had lost her mind, and they all backed up away from her. She, very ceremoniously, laid her hands upon the engine of the truck and commanded it to start in the name of Jesus. She got done speaking the word of authority, and told the man: "turn the key, and the pickup truck will start." They looked at each other, like, "we got a real nut case on our hands." So, one of the men reluctantly got into the truck and turned the key. Guess what? ... Nothing happened!

Once again, she laid her hands upon the engine and commanded it to start in Jesus name! Again, she told the man to try it. He turned the key. Guess what? Nothing happened! This went on for a while, until the men finally got fed up with her and basically told her to mind her own business. She walked away from this ordeal extremely discouraged. The man she had tried to minister to, she had actually more spiritually hurt than helped.

Why did this happen? Because she did not have the Word of the Lord to do this. Yes, we can lay hands on the sick, but I find there are times when the Holy Spirit tells me not to. Yes, we should share the gospel with those we meet. But there are times when the Holy Spirit tells me not to.

Pastor Mike: Can you prove this is in the Bible? Yes! Look at the life of Jesus! He stepped over all the sick, infirmed, and crippled people to get to one man lying on a cot, at the pool of Bethesda. He also walked by the man at the Beautiful Gate every day without healing him. But one day, as Peter was going by this man (as he usually did) he had a quickening in his heart that the man was ready to be healed: "Silver and Gold Have I Not" said Peter: "But such as I have give I thee, **In the Name of Jesus Christ of Nazareth,** get up and walk!" Instantly the man received healing into his feet and ankle-bones. He leaped up and began to dance and praise the Lord.

Why didn't Jesus or Peter heal this man before this time? Because the Father did not tell them to. When the Father Speaks - Is When We Jump to It And Do What He Tells Us to Do! Then we will get the results that we so much desire. We must be in the right place to hear the voice of God.

1 Samuel 15:22 And Samuel said, Hath the LORD as great delight in burnt offerings and sacrifices, as in obeying the voice of the LORD? Behold, to obey is better than sacrifice, and to hearken than the fat of rams.

#6 GOD TAUGHT ME HOW TO LIVE BY VIOLENT FAITH! (1975)

God, Where Are You?

This Little Teaching Could Save Your Life!

In our walk with God, there are many things that we absolutely must learn. I wish that we could instantly learn them - just from reading the Bible. But … this is not the case. I had to learn a very hard lesson early in my Christian walk, one that many believers who have walked with God for years still have not learned.

I believe the reason that I had to learn this lesson was because of the amount of trials, tests and hardships that I was to experience throughout my lifetime. I had to learn how to not live by feelings, or by the circumstances that surrounded me.

I gave my heart to Christ on February 18th, 1975

My whole life before this had been filled with pain, sorrow, depression, low self-esteem, physical disabilities, etc. You name it, I had it. But when I gave my heart to Christ, I was instantly overwhelmed by the presence of God. It was like electricity going through my body, twenty-four hours a day, seven days a week. This did not go away, but continued upon me.

I was instantly set free from all addictions, as well as emotional and mental problems. I was a brand-new creation in Christ Jesus. I fell in love with my Lord: head over heels. I immediately began devouring the Word of the Living God; specifically the four Gospels. I got filled with the Holy Ghost, healed, and I preached my first sermon very shortly after I was saved. I think I took the presence and touch of God upon my life for granted, at that time, as if that was the normal, everyday experience, for every believer. I was soon to discover this was not true.

One morning I got up early to pray and read my Bible - as normal - but something was wrong. I had grown used to the very tangible presence and manifestation of God but, to my shock and horror, it was gone! I mean, to me, personally ... the presence of God was gone. Confusion suddenly clouded my heart and my mind. I cried out to God: "Lord, what's wrong? How have I offended you?" I did not hear any answer, which was, to me, also very strange. The Lord was constantly speaking to my heart. I examined myself to see if there was something I was doing that was against the will of God. I could not find anything wrong. I didn't know what else to do and I didn't really have anyone that I could go to, at that time, who was mature enough to help me.

So, I kept reading my Bible, kept on praying, worshipping, praising and sharing Christ as I went along. I went to bed that night with no sense of God's presence. The next morning I got up early, hoping that His presence had come back, but to my shock and sadness, God was not there. Once again, I went through the torment of examining my heart, crying out to Jesus and following my regular routine throughout the day. I went to bed that night in the same condition.

During the whole experience, I did not back off or give up but just kept pressing in.

This went on, day after day, after day. God just was not there in His tangible presence. Yes, I did get depressed, but I did not give up. I did not stop praying or reading my Bible. I never ceased worshiping and praising God. I did not stop sharing my faith with others and telling them the wonderful things Jesus had done for me. I think approximately two weeks went by with me in this spiritual desert —a no man's land— a dark and dry place in my daily walk. I did not know what was wrong, and there was nothing else I could do but keep pressing in closer. After about two weeks, I went to bed one night, praying and talking to God, even though He was not answering me in the same way as He did before.

The next morning I got up early and began to pray ... when out of the blue God's presence came rushing in stronger than ever - like a mighty wind. It was like a powerful tsunami, a forceful flood of His presence and His Spirit. God's touch was upon me greatly. I began to laugh, to cry and to shout. Oh! It was so good to have God with me again.

I said to the Lord, when I was finally able to talk: "Lord, where were you?" There seemed to be a long pause, then He said to me, with what seemed to be a bit of amusement in His voice: **"I Was Here All Along."**

"You were, Lord?" **He replied: "Yes."** Then He said something that would forever change my life: **"I was teaching you how to live by faith."** He began to very specifically teach me out of the Scriptures, that man does not live by bread alone but by every word that comes out of the mouth of God.

Matthew 4:4 But he answered and said, It is written, Man shall not live by bread alone, but by every word that proceedeth out of the mouth of God.

I learned that our walk with Him does not depend upon our feelings, emotions, location or circumstances. And that many of those who are believers are destroyed by the enemy because they do not understand nor believe this. Even the Apostle Paul had to learn how to be content in Christ, in whatever condition, trusting God, knowing that He is not a man that He should lie. Christ said that He would never leave us nor forsake us. We may call upon Christ with a sincere heart: knowing that He will be there for us, to answer us and show us great and mighty things which we know not!

Over forty years have come and gone since I learned this lesson. I now no longer allow the feelings of either His absence or His presence to affect me. Of course, I constantly examine my heart, but if I can find nothing wrong, I simply realize that I am flying by instruments and no longer operating by visual flight rules **(VFR).** Thank God, as the aviation industry would say, I am SFR rated! There are two sets of regulations governing all aspects of civilian aircraft operations: the first is Instrument flight rules **(IFR)** and the second is visual flight rules **(VFR)** defined as flying by sight and sensory input. All Christians are to be rated as (SFR) which would equate to Spiritual Flight Rules!

#7 Devil Worshiper Delivered By the Power of God!
(1975)

My first encounter with a demon-possessed man was in 1975. I had only been a Christian for about two months, and I was in the Navy at the time. I was stationed on a military base on Adak, Alaska. One night (at about 8 p.m.) I was witnessing in my dormitory room to three men doing Bible study.

While sharing biblical truths with these three men, another man entered my room. We called him T.J. This individual had always been very different - and strange. He was kind of out there! I had never even spoken to him, up to that time, except one night when he showed a nasty movie to the guys in his dorm. I had walked out of his room, not being able to handle his level of filth!

When T.J. entered my room, he took over my Bible study and began to preach some weird, off-the-wall things about the devil. He said he was from California where he had been part of a satanic church. He showed us the ends of his fingers in which some of the ends were missing from the first joint out. He told us that he had eaten them for power, and he had drunk human blood at satanic worship services. As he spoke, there seemed to be an invisible power speaking through him. An evil and demonic darkness descended upon us in my dormitory. A visible, demonic power took him over, right in front of our eyes, and his eyes filled with a malevolent glow! One of the guys in my room, Hussein, (who was a Muslim) declared this was too much for him, and left the room. The other two, Bobby and Willie, sat and listened.

I had never encountered anything as sinister and evil as this ever before. I honestly didn't know what to do (at that time) so I went downstairs to the barracks right below me. There was a fellow Christian I'd had the opportunity of working with, who lived right below me. After I had given my heart to Jesus Christ, Willie, the cowboy, told me that he too was a born again, Spirit-filled Christian. I had yet to see the evidence of this in Willie's life, but I didn't know where else to go. I went down to his room and knocked on Willie's door. When he opened the door, I explained to him what was happening in my room.

I was able to get him to go to my room. Willie stepped into my dormitory and stopped. We both saw that T.J. was now up on a stool, made from a log, and he was preaching under the power of satanic spirits. At that very moment, cowboy Willie turned tail and ran out of my room. I went after him! He told me that he had no idea what to do and that he could not handle this. He left me standing outside my door. Alone.

I went back into my room and did the only thing I could do: I **Cried out to Jesus Christ**. The minute I cried out, looking up towards heaven, I'm telling you, a bright light from heaven shone right through my ceiling. It was a beam of light about three feet wide, an all glistening bright light, shining upon me. I do not know if anyone else in my room saw the bright light. All I know is that the Spirit of God rose up within me, and I was overwhelmed with God's presence.

My mouth was instantly filled with an amazingly powerful and Prophetic Word from Heaven. I began to preach Jesus Christ by the Power of the Spirit! As I began to speak by the Spirit, the power of God fell in that room. The next thing I knew, T.J. had dropped to the floor, like a rock. T.J. began squirming just like a snake; his body bending and twisting in an impossible way. There was no fear left in my heart as I watched this demonic activity. There was nothing but a Holy Ghost boldness and divine inspiration flowing through me at that time.

During this divine encounter of Heaven, both Willie and Bobby had fallen on their knees, crying out to Jesus to save them. At the same time, they gave their hearts to the Lord, and they were both instantly filled with the Holy Ghost! The next thing I knew, I found myself kneeling over the top of T.J. as he was squirming like a snake. I placed my hands upon him. Willie and Bobby came over and joined me, they also laid their hands upon T.J. With a voice of authority, inspired by the Spirit, I commanded the demons to come out of the man in the Name of Jesus Christ. As God is my witness, we all heard three to five different voices come screaming out of T.J.!

When the demons were gone, it was like T.J. breathed a last, long, breath, like that of a dying man, and he was completely still. After a while, he opened up his eyes - now filled with complete peace. At that very moment, he gave his heart to Jesus Christ. I led him into the baptism of the Holy Ghost. The presence of God overwhelmed all of us as we gave praise and thanks to the Lord. The next Sunday these three men went with me to church.

Evil Personified

T.J. the man I had cast the demons out of, came to my room one night. His heart was filled with great fear, because he had been so deeply involved in the satanic realm. He was hearing satanic voices telling him that they were going to kill him. One night as I was sleeping, T.J. began to scream. He was yelling that the devil was there to kill him! I sat up in my bunk and looked around. From the position of my bed, I saw the light of the moon shining through our big plate glass window. There, on our wall, was a shadow of a large, demonic entity. I was not making this up.

This entity moved across the room towards T.J. The very atmosphere of the room was filled with a terrible presence of evil. Fear tried to rise within my heart, but the Spirit of God quickened courage and boldness within me. I rose up out of my bed, commanded this demonic power to leave our room and never return in the name of Jesus Christ of Nazareth. The minute I spoke to it in the name of Jesus, I heard a screeching voice, like fingernails scraping across a chalk board. The shadow was pulled out of the room, as if a gigantic vacuum cleaner had been turned on, and it was being sucked up by an invisible force. This demonic power never came back again.

Romans 4:18 Who against hope believed in hope, that he might become the father of many nations; according to that which was spoken, So shall thy seed be.

#8 Typical Missionary Journey

I arrived in the Philippines with some kind of stomach flu, or virus, and I became deathly sick. On top of the sickness, I was extremely tired because of jet lag. The trip over was a nightmare! I had used a foreign airline to get a low price, but you get what you pay for. It was a crowded flight, with babies crying and filling their diapers. The air in the airplane was extremely hot and stuffy; it stunk so bad that I almost had to breathe through my shirt. The seats on the plane were very small and uncomfortable. The person sitting next to me was practically sitting on my lap! The journey was almost twenty-four hours long. When I arrived in Manila, I had to catch another small plane which would take me to the province of Samar, to the town of Calbayog City. I waited about four hours before I boarded the small plane to get to Calbayog.

When I landed at the airport in Calbayog, I had to take what they call a Jeepney, which looks like a Willies Jeep, only it's about ten times bigger. I had to ride this Jeep, crowded with other travelers, all the way out to where I was to meet up with the believers I was working with. There are no windows in the Jeepney - except for the very front windshield. Because of this, I breathed in diesel fuel for hours while traveling on rough, bouncy roads. Filipinos were pushing up against me all the way. I felt like an animal crowded in a cage.

After more than thirty hours without sleep my head was throbbing so bad I could hardly handle it. I felt like I was going to pass out at any minute. I was sicker then sick. Finally, after what felt like a never-ending nightmare, I arrived at Catarman, where I was scheduled to preach. In the natural, I was in no condition to preach or minister. Yet, I made it to my first meeting. The building had a tin roof, walls made of block, and the seats were wooden benches with no backs.

I almost fell over, right then and there, but I buckled down and gritted my teeth. When it was time for me to speak, the Spirit of God quickened my mortal flesh. I preached like a house on fire! For the next twenty days, nonstop, I preached every chance they gave me. My mind, heart, and body were energized and quickened by the Holy Ghost. This is the life of **Violent faith!**

James 1:2-4 My brethren, count it all joy when ye fall into divers temptations; 3 Knowing this, that the trying of your faith worketh patience. 4 But let patience have her perfect work, that ye may be perfect and entire, wanting nothing.

A Brief Description of Faith:

When God, His Word and His will are Supernaturally Quickened to you by the Holy Spirit! These realities become more real to you than anything in life. It is a revelation of who Jesus Christ & God, the Father really are! What They have done and Are doing. It is a quickening in your heart, when you know, that you know, that you know, that you know: if God is with you, then who can be against you? Christ Jesus, Himself, lives inside of you. Your mind, your will, your emotions, and every part of your being is overwhelmed with the reality of Jesus Christ! And you enter into the realm where all things are possible! This is where, by God's grace, it is my hope and desire to take you.

CHAPTER THREE

Violent Faith Comes By Hearing Jesus Christ Preached And Exalted!

Romans 10:13-15 For whosoever shall call upon the name of the Lord shall be saved. 14 How then shall they call on <u>him</u> in whom they have not believed? and how shall they believe in <u>him</u> of whom they have not heard? and how shall they hear without a preacher? 15 And how shall they preach, except they be sent? as it is written, How beautiful are the feet of them that preach the gospel of peace, and bring glad tidings of good things!

We need to begin this very important **truth, in which this Audacious Faith comes**, by looking at Romans chapter 10 - starting with verse 13: *"Whosoever shall call upon the name of the Lord shall be saved!"* The word, *'whosoever'* is important because **Jesus** also said: *"whosoever shall say unto this mountain!"* 1 John: 4-5 says: *"for whatsoever is born of God overcomes the world: and this is the victory that overcomes the world, even our faith. Who is he that OVERCOMES the world, but he that believe that* **Jesus Christ is the son of God.***"*

We are talking about the subject of faith in **Christ**. **Jesus** said that He did not come to destroy. He said: *"I am come that you might have life and have it more abundantly!" John 10:10* He was talking about His people - those called by His name. He wants you to have life and have it more abundantly. The Greek word used for 'life' here is: 'Zoe' or 'life as God has it.' God wants His divine life operating in you and me, but there are a lot of people in the church (the body) that are not experiencing this abundant life. The reason why they are not experiencing this abundant life is because they are not walking by faith.

They are walking by their feelings, emotions, circumstances and situations. Slaves of their five senses and the elements of the world. They are not walking or living by faith - yet **Christ** wants us to have life and have it more abundantly. It can only be done by **the one who comes** to God. And he/she must believe that God is a rewarder of those who diligently seek **Him.** Now we need to take a look at *Romans 10:17* - this is the **way that audacious faith comes:**

So then faith cometh by hearing, and hearing by the word of God.

This particular verse is used, quite often, by people who are under the misconception that this is the only way that faith comes. Even the way they interpret it is basically wrong. In order to properly understand this Scripture, we must keep it in context. Let's look at what it says in *Hebrews 11:6*:

But without faith it is impossible to please him: for he that cometh to God must believe that he is, and that he is a rewarder of them that diligently seek him.

Notice that if you truly believe - **YOU** will come to God! **He that cometh to God must believe, and if you believe, you will come.** You will pursue God because your faith is alive and active. Thereby, you will seek the face of God if He is working in you. You will go after God like a deer after water - in a dry and thirsty land. To fully grasp this concept we must look at *Romans 10:13: For whosoever shall call upon the name of the Lord shall be saved!*

I want to emphasize the word '**Lord**!' We are talking about the **Lord Jesus.** *Romans 10:14: How shall they believe in <u>him</u> of whom they have not heard? And how shall they hear without a preacher?* So really, the context of this particular declaration in Romans is that faith comes by hearing; and hearing by the **Word of God** - out of the mouth of a preacher. Notice that it did not say, 'faith cometh by reading, faith cometh by you hearing yourself.' That is a totally different subject. This Scripture says that faith comes by hearing from a preacher. Then it tells us something about the preacher in *Romans 10:15:*

And how shall they preach, except they be sent? as it is written, How beautiful are the feet of them that preach the gospel of peace, and bring glad tidings of good things!

Audacious, Holy, and Violent Faith comes by hearing. And hearing by the preaching of a minister of the gospel who is under the divine influence of the Holy Ghost - speaking by the Holy Spirit.

This is a very important declaration! **Jesus** said: "*my words are spirit and they are life.*" For faith to be ministered by the preaching of the Word, it must be done by a man who is **operating in true, authentic, living, active and dynamic faith.**

Romans 10:17 So then faith cometh by hearing, and hearing by the word of God.

Another translation does not say: "the word of God" but says: "*by the declaration of Jesus Christ!*"

I will prove that biblical faith comes by hearing the proclamation of **Jesus Christ**! Faith comes by the preaching of **Jesus Christ**: who **Jesus Christ** is, what **Jesus Christ** has done, and what He is about to do! Please see the message of *Romans 10:6-11:*

45

But the righteousness which is of faith speaketh on this wise, Say not in thine heart, who shall ascend into heaven? (that is, to bring Christ down from above:) 7 Or, Who shall descend into the deep? (that is, to bring up Christ again from the dead.) 8 But what saith it? The word is nigh thee, even in thy mouth, and in thy heart: that is, the word of faith, which we preach; 9 That if thou shalt confess with thy mouth the Lord Jesus, and shalt believe in thine heart that God hath raised him from the dead, thou shalt be saved. 10 For with the heart man believeth unto righteousness; and with the mouth confession is made unto salvation. 11 For the scripture saith, Whosoever believeth on him shall not be ashamed.

Not every minister preaches the **Word of Faith - which is Jesus Christ**! Okay, so you need to have the name of **Jesus Christ** on your lips, and believe in your heart that **Jesus Christ** is **Lord**, and that God raised **Him from the dead**. We who preach **Jesus Christ** must believe that **He Overcame** principalities, powers and made a show of the devil and demons; triumphing over them in it! And the minister must have made **Jesus** Lord of his life.

The **Word of Faith** that I preach and believe, WILL cause **Jesus** to be Lord over my life. **Jesus** IS Lord of my hands. **Jesus** IS Lord of my thoughts. **Jesus** IS Lord of my feet. **Jesus** IS Lord of my heart. **Jesus** IS Lord of my emotions. **Jesus** IS Lord of my feelings. **Jesus** IS Lord of my circumstances. **Jesus** IS Lord of my eyes. **Jesus** IS Lord of my finances. In every area of my life: He MUST BE **Lord**! As ministers, if we have truly made **Jesus** the **Lord** of our life, then as we preach, the words we speak will be filled with the Spirit and Power of **Christ**.

John 6:63 It is the spirit that quickeneth; the flesh profiteth nothing: the words that I speak unto you, they are spirit, and they are life.

Faith comes by hearing, and hearing by the declaration of who Jesus Christ is; from the lips of a person who has been enabled, by the ability of God, to preach Jesus Christ. A person who has made Jesus Lord of their life, thereby the spirit of faith is released into the hearts of the hearers!

#9 A Vision Of Jesus & His Stripes (1975)

I was reading my **Bible**, as a brand new believer, when I discovered that Jesus Christ went about healing all who were sick and oppressed of the devil. I began to search the Scriptures on this particular subject, and as I studied, I discovered many Scriptures that supported this:

Isaiah 53:4-5 Surely he hath borne our griefs, and carried our sorrows: yet we did esteem him stricken, smitten of God, and afflicted. 5 But he was wounded for our transgressions, he was bruised for our iniquities: the chastisement of our peace was upon him; and with his stripes we are healed.

1 Peter 2:24 Who his own self bare our sins in his own body on the tree, that we, being dead to sins, should live unto righteousness: by whose stripes ye were healed.

Matthew 8:16-17 When the even was come, they brought unto him many that were possessed with devils: and he cast out the spirits with his word, and healed all that were sick: 17 That it might be fulfilled which was spoken by Esaias the prophet, saying, Himself took our infirmities, and bare our sicknesses.

As I read and **meditated** upon these Scriptures, something happened within my heart. Great, overwhelming sorrow took a hold of me as I first saw the pain and the agony that Jesus went through for my healing. **In my heart and in my mind I saw that He had taken my sicknesses and my diseases.** I experienced a great love for the Son of God and the price He paid for my healing.

Then it **Happened!** It was like an open vision in which I saw my precious **Lord** and **Saviour** tied to the whipping post. I saw the Roman soldiers striking the back of **Jesus** with the whips. I saw the flesh and blood of my precious **Lord** sprinkling everything within its range, with each terrible strike of the soldiers' whip. I wept because I knew this was done for me. Even to this day, when I retell this story, great love and sorrow fills my heart; yet I also have great joy, because I know that by the stripes of **Jesus I am healed**.

In that moment, something **Exploded Within My Heart**: an amazing revelation that I no longer have to be sick! In the **name of Jesus** I would not allow what my **Lord** went through to be for nothing. I would no longer allow sickness and disease to dwell in my body, which is the temple of the Holy Ghost.

Jesus had taken my sicknesses and my diseases. No ifs, ands, or buts. No matter what it looked like, or how I felt, I knew within my heart that **Jesus Christ** had set me free from all demonic afflictions relating to sickness and disease. **Anger!!** Yes! A great anger, rose up in my heart against the enemy of my Lord. The demonic world has no right to afflict me or any other believer because **Jesus Christ** took our sicknesses and bore our diseases.

I had been born with terrible physical infirmities. I found myself speaking out loud, with authority, to my ears and commanded them to be open (and normal) in the name of Jesus

Christ of Nazareth. I then spoke to my lungs and commanded them to be healed in the name of Jesus Christ of Nazareth. Next, I commanded my sinuses to be delivered, so that I could smell normal scents, in the name of Jesus Christ of Nazareth.

The minute I spoke the Word of God to my physical man, my ears popped completely open. Up to that moment I'd had significant hearing loss, but as I was listening to Christian music playing softly (or at least I thought it was!) the music became so loud that I had to turn it down. Furthermore, my lungs were clear and I haven't experienced any lung congestion since! I used to be so allergic to dust that I would literally end up in an oxygen tent in the hospital. My mother had to work extra hard to keep our house dust-free. From that moment - to date – dust and mold allergies, or any such thing has never come back to torment me or cause any problems. What's more, my sense of smell returned instantly! I had broken my nose about four times due to fights, accidents, and rough activities and I could barely smell anything.

Suddenly, I could smell a terrible odour. I tried to find out where it was coming from … then I looked at my feet. I wondered if it could be them? I put my foot on a nightstand and bent over toward it. I took a big sniff and nearly fell over. Man! Did my feet stink!! I went straight over to the bathroom and washed them in the sink.

Acts 10:38 How God anointed Jesus of Nazareth with the Holy Ghost and with power: who went about doing good, and healing all that were oppressed of the devil; for God was with him.

For over forty years I have aggressively, violently and persistently, taken a hold of my healing!

I refuse to let the devil rob me of what Jesus so painfully purchased. It is mine! The devil cannot have it. The thought has never even entered my mind to go and see a doctor when physical sickness attacks my body, for I already have a doctor, His name is Jesus Christ of Nazareth. He is the Great Physician and He has already healed me with His stripes.

Yes ... there have been times when the manifestation of my healing seemed like it would never come. But I know, that I know, that I know, by His stripes I am healed. Strong faith never considers the circumstances.

Romans 4:18-20 Who against hope believed in hope, that he might become the father of many nations, according to that which was spoken, So shall thy seed be. 19 And being not weak in faith, he considered not his own body now dead, when he was about an hundred years old, neither yet the deadness of Sarah's womb: 20 He staggered not at the promise of God through unbelief; but was strong in faith, giving glory to God;

One of my most common declarations is: "If I Were, Then I Was, And If I Was, Then I Am, If I Am, Then I Is - I Is Healed!"

WE ARE ON THE EDGE OF A GREAT AWAKENING!

As a Minister of the Gospel since 1975, the number one missing element that I have seen in most believers lives is the **WORD of GOD**. God has given to us the Supernatural Weapon of His Word; it is to be hidden in our heart and spoken out of our mouth. Those who have taken the time to hide God's Word in their heart have experienced many miracles. Yet, I say there is so much more.

Through the years I have seen God marvelously deliver, heal, provide, protect and manifest Himself in my life as I have given myself to Prayer in His Word. Yet there is so much more! If we will pay the price, come out of the darkness, and completely immerse ourselves in the **TRUTH of HIS WORD**, we will move into the realm where All Things Are Possible!

As I shared with you - at the beginning of this book – back in 2013 I was sleeping when I heard the Audible Voice of God say to me: **"The Violent Take It by Force!"** It was around three o'clock in the morning and I instantly awoke out of a deep sleep. My heart trembled, and I knew what the Lord was saying. You see, through the years I have experienced many visitations and manifestations of God in my life. This is by no means an exaggeration or self-exaltation: God Chooses to 'Use the Foolish to Confound the Wise'.

One of the Major Keys to all of my experiences (I would not take $1million to trade any of them) is God's Word is hidden in my heart. Yet there is so much more that God has for all of us. I Prophesy that we are on the edge of a **Great Awakening**! What will this **Great Awakening** be? It will be a Divine Hunger that will come Exploding into the heart of the Bride of Jesus. It will be a love For **God's Word**! *Psalm 119:97 Oh how love I thy law! it is my meditation all the day.*

Jeremiah 15:16 Thy words were found, and I did eat them; and thy word was unto me the joy and rejoicing of mine heart:

This Divine Encounter with the Audible Voice of God was Him motivating me to eat, and drink more of **HIS** flesh and **HIS** blood! It Is the Word of God hidden in my heart. The time is upon us when the Bride, The Holy Church of Jesus Christ will become obsessed with the Word of God. *1 John 5:3: "For this is the love of God, that we keep his commandments: And his commandments are not grievous."* I Prophesy that a new love for God's Word is about to come upon His Church. His People. His Beloved.

John 6:53-56 Then Jesus said unto them, Verily, verily, I say unto you, Except ye eat the flesh of the Son of man, and drink his blood, ye have no life in you. 54 Whoso eateth my flesh, and drinketh my blood, hath eternal life; and I will raise him up at the last day. 55 For my flesh is meat indeed, and my blood is drink indeed. 56 He that eateth my flesh, and drinketh my blood, dwelleth in me, and I in him.

#10 Brain-Quickening Experience.

Around 1995, the Lord basically told me that I was a "favorite scripture" preacher and that I really did not know His Word the way I should. I was so convicted by this confrontation from God that I made a commitment to myself: whenever I got home from a meeting I would begin to pour myself into the Bible, like I should. I was going to spend hours **in God's Word** and in prayer.

I informed my staff (I had twenty-one people working for me) that I would begin to give myself to long hours of prayer and the Word. I began with the book of Ephesians, and started with the very first chapter. I not only wanted to memorize it, I wanted to get it deep into my heart. It took me close to three weeks and countless hours to memorize. **This was violent faith at work within my heart**.

The next mountain I climbed was the book of Galatians. As I memorized the Scriptures and chapters of the Bible I experienced tremendous headaches. But … I kept working at it because I knew that without pain - there is no gain!

Once I had conquered the book of Galatians, I moved on to Philippians. As I got into the second chapter of Philippians, something Supernatural took place. I had what the Bible calls an

'Open Vision.' This happens when you are wide-awake and everything disappears - except what God is showing you.

Right there in front of me was a large body of crystal-clear water: pure blue with not one ripple on it. It stretched as far as the natural eye could see; in every direction. The room I was in had all but disappeared and there was nothing but a gigantic, blue lake. I lifted up my head and looked into a beautiful, light-blue, cloudless sky. I saw a large, crystal-clear raindrop falling down from the heavens in slow-motion. I watched in amazement as it slowly tumbled down towards the lake. When it hit the surface of the water it caused ripples to flow forth.

The ripples flowed from the center of the water, where the drop had hit, and began to grow in size and intensity. Then … all of a sudden the vision was over. It ended as quickly as it began. I stood there in amazement, not understanding what had just happened. I knew this experience was from God, but I did not know what its significance was.

I knew in my heart that eventually God would show me what the vision meant. You see, when the Lord gives me a supernatural visitation, I do not lean on the understanding of my natural mind. I just simply give it to the Lord, knowing that in His time He will show me what He meant - or what He was saying.

When the vision ended, I picked up my Bible to get back to memorizing the Scriptures and I immediately noticed there was a change in my mental capacity. It seemed like my brain was absorbing the Word of God like a sponge. Amazingly, within one hour, I'd memorized a whole chapter - as if it were nothing! To my total surprise I'd developed a photographic memory! Before the vision it took me days to memorize a chapter, and now I could memorize a chapter in one hour!! I continued to memorize books of the Bible until there were ten books inside of me. This is not including the thousands of other Scriptures that I continued to memorize when dealing with certain subjects (I have videos on YouTube where I quote whole books of the Bible by memory).

Why in the world would God open up my heart and my mind the way He did to memorize the Word? The Word of God has the capacity to quicken our minds and mortal bodies. God's Word is awesome, quick and powerful. There is an activation of the things of the Spirit when we begin to give ourselves one-hundred percent into whatever it is God has called us to do. There is a dynamic principle of laying down our lives in order to release the aroma, the presence, and the power of heaven.

I'm sorry to say that I became so busy with running the church, a Christian school, a small Bible college, a radio station, TV broadcasting and construction projects and twenty-five churches in the Philippines - not including other aspects of being a pastor - that I did not continue to memorize the Bible. I know within my heart that if I'd continued on a complete diet of God's Word and saturated my whole being with the truth, I would have been able to accomplish a thousand times more than what I have. Thank God that I'm still alive, that I still have breath, and this opportunity is still before both you and I.

Even though I did not continue to saturate myself with the Word of God, through the years, I have continued in His Word on a daily basis. You see, I've had an insatiable hunger for the Word of God ever since I was saved. As a result of God's Word in my heart, the Lord has allowed me to write over seven-thousand sermons and forty books. I have also been able to do many things that I have never been taught or trained to do. Furthermore, in the midst of all these activities I earned a Ph.D. in Biblical Theology and I received a Doctorate of Divinity. I believe it is all because of the divine, supernatural visitations and quickenings of God's Holy Spirit. The reason why I believe we do not experience more visitations is because of a lack of spiritual hunger, prayer, and God's Word hidden in our hearts. If we would hunger and thirst, God would satisfy these desires.

#11 Precious Lady Delivered from Seizures (1979)

My wife and I completed Bible college and moved back to Pennsylvania to pastor a small church. God put it upon my heart to pay off the debt of this church (independent), and to close it down so that it would not leave a bad witness in the community. Once this was completed we began to attend different churches - as the Spirit of God led us. One Sunday morning my wife and I attended an Assembly of God Church in Three Springs, Pennsylvania. As the pastor was preaching there was a commotion about six pews in front of us.

A woman (probably in her late 30s) had gone into a terrible epileptic seizure. She had fallen off her pew, and was now laying in the aisle between the pews: kicking and flailing about. What was so strange is that everybody in the church ignored her, and the pastor kept preaching - like everything was normal. My wife and I looked at each other wondering what in the world was going on. I asked the lady next to us (in a whisper) what was happening? She whispered back that this lady had seizures all the time, and there was nothing they could do. Everybody had simply learned just to act like nothing was wrong.

I could not believe what I was hearing! There was no way that I was going to sit and watch this woman tormented by the devil while the pastor continued to preach. I whispered to my wife that I would be right back and got up out of my pew. I walked up to where the woman was (she was still on the floor having the seizure) and I bent down to put my hands on her squirming body. **I whispered: "you Foul spirit in the name of Jesus Christ loose her. Right Now!"**

I removed my hands and waited for the manifestation of my command to be fulfilled. Within less than one-minute she stopped squirming, her eyes refocused, and she was okay. I helped her to get up and then sat her down. Her mouth and face were covered with spit and saliva and I could tell that this particular lady was not altogether there mentally. When I was done helping her, I went back to my pew.

The whole time the congregation just went on with the service, and the pastor kept on preaching. Even though this woman desperately needed help - they had not helped her. Why? I believe it is because they did not understand the authority that we have in Jesus Christ when we are fully submitted to God. But that is not the end of the story. Not long after, the pastor of that particular church moved on to another church. Therefore, the church needed a new pastor. My wife's grandmother was a member of the church and she informed me that they were looking for a new pastor. I told her that because I was not an Assembly of God minister they would not be able to hire me. In the midst of me explaining this to Kathy's grandmother, the Lord spoke to my heart, and told me I would be the next pastor.

Arrangements were made, and I sat down with the church board letting them know that I would be glad to fill-in, and preach for them until they found another pastor. I did not tell them that God had spoken to my heart and informed me that I would be their next pastor. That was God's job, not mine! They had me come and minister, and God moved mightily in every one of the services. The next thing I knew, they asked me to be their pastor. However, because I was not an Assembly of God minister, I would have to go before those who were in charge of our district. I agreed to do this. The man who was over the Pennsylvania district was located in Camp Hill Pennsylvania. His name was Philip Bongiorno and he was the Superintendent of the Pennsylvania and Delaware District of the Assemblies of God.

I arrived on the prearranged date to speak with the Superintendent. He was an elderly man, and I could tell he had a deep relationship with God. He asked me questions about my life, my experiences, and my education. When I was done speaking, and had answered all his questions, he simply looked at me and said: "I Never Interfere with What God Is Doing!" He shook my hand and informed me that I was the new pastor of Three Springs Assembly Of God Church.

Now, back to my story about Norma, the woman tormented with epileptic seizures; as long as I was pastor at Three Springs, I never allowed the devil to manifest himself in my services again and Norma never had another seizure. Before each service I prayed with her and took authority over the demonic spirits afflicting her life. I also told Norma that we could help her become free. My wife and I sat down with Norma and asked her when the seizures began. She informed us that when she was a little girl she'd had a terrible accident and had damaged her head. As a result of the accident she'd been taken to the hospital and doctors had to perform an operation on her. The doctors told Norma's parents that there was a buildup of water on her brain and they had to drill down into her skull in order to get to the buildup and release the pressure.

The operation did succeed in this regards, but, with two bad results. Firstly: from that moment forward she was never the same mentally. Her mind had never completely fully developed and she was slow in speech, and slow in her actions. She was no simpleton, but her mind simply never developed. Secondly: she had terrible seizures all the time. No matter what medication they gave her, it did not seem to be able to stop these seizures.

I told Norma that I would pray about her situation. I'm sorry to say that I had ministers come through our church who prayed for Norma and prophesied that she would never have another seizure again - after they had prayed for her. Their prophecies proved to be false because the seizures continued. As I sought the Lord about Norma's situation, He informed me that Norma was not demon-possessed, (which I knew) but demonic powers did come upon her, at different times, to oppress her. The Lord gave me specific instructions on how to help Norma overcome the seizures. We sat her down again, and asked her if she could tell when the seizures were going to happen.

In the beginning, she said that she could not tell, and there were no warning signs. We went a little deeper with the questions and I asked her if, at times, she got confused, upset, disorientated, or aggravated. She sat for a while thinking about my question. Eventually she said: "Yes. Now that you have asked me this question, I do seem to get confused, or aggravated and disorientated right before I have a seizure."

I replied: "Okay Norma, this is what I want you to do. The next time these emotions and feelings begin to come upon you, I want you to stop everything right then and there. Take the name of Jesus and say: "In the Name of Jesus Christ I command you devil to go from me now, In Jesus Name!" I said: "Norma keep saying In Jesus Name, In Jesus Name, In Jesus Name! Keep saying it to yourself until all of the feelings of confusion, aggravation, disorientation, or anger leave." She agreed that she would do this. Now, throughout the week I would usually receive phone calls from Norma's family asking us to pray because she'd had a terrible seizure. All that week we did not hear another word about her. When she came to church on the next Sunday she was filled with great joy. She informed us that she had not had any seizures because she had followed my directions. She'd had a week free from seizures - which was so absolutely amazing and wonderful for her!

There were times when she still had seizures, but she informed us it was whenever she did not use the name of Jesus quickly enough when she was being hit with feelings of confusion, frustration, disorientation, or anger. After this she ran into another challenge: instead of having seizures during the day, she began to have very terrible seizures in her sleep. She was devastated by the fact that she was not yet free. I told her, by the Spirit of God, that if she took authority over the demonic powers before going to sleep the seizures would not happen to her. She agreed to take the name of Jesus and bind the enemy before she went to bed. To her great delight, when she remembered to use her authority over the enemy: In the Name of Jesus, when she went to bed - the seizures never returned. I later left that church to be a missionary in Europe. However, the last time we saw Norma, she was still free of the seizures.

Whom the Son Sets Free Is Free Indeed!

CHAPTER FOUR

You Have To Meditate Upon The Word!

If you study the Book of Romans, chapter 10, in context - it is literally talking about the preaching of **Jesus Christ**! When ministers preach **Jesus Christ** - from a heart filled with faith - that faith becomes **contagious**. This is why we need to preach **Jesus Christ**. It is all about **Jesus**! Through Him. To Him. By Him. This is why in the New Testament, from Matthew to the end of the Book of Revelation, (about 163 pages and 7,957 Scriptures) **Jesus Christ** Himself is referred to, in a personal and intimate way, more than **9000** times!

At this moment in time, we are living in a physical world with our feet on the ground. Planet Earth - where we live - is spinning around The Sun. The Moon is spinning around The Earth. We also have Mercury, Jupiter, Mars, Venus, and all the other planets spinning around The Sun too. Now, we call the invisible power behind this: "gravitation." Gravitation is an amazing, invisible force that scientists still do not fully understand. I believe the invisible force we call "gravitation" is **God's faith** manifested. Scripture declares that **God upholds all things by the Word of His Power.** In the New Testament we can go to any chapter and discover the subject of faith! Why? Because it is all about faith in **Jesus Christ!**

Acts 17:28 For in him we live, and move, and have our being; as certain also of your own poets have said, For we are also his offspring.

In the Book of Romans, chapter 12, we see **How Radical Faith Comes**. But first, I need to give you a word of warning! Let's look at *Romans 14:22:*

Hast thou faith? have it to thyself before God. Happy is he that condemneth not himself in that thing which he alloweth.

Our faith in God is not dependent upon any other person. By faith, we can go as high and as deep in God as we want. Romans 14:22 is a warning about the Sabbath days, the holy days and meats. It makes known the convictions of people and what they perceive to be the will of God. The danger here, is that we can have convictions about what we believe is the will of God - when it is not His will at all – and we have to live under these convictions because anything that is not of faith is sin.

1 Timothy 4:3-5 Forbidding to marry, and commanding to abstain from meats, which God hath created to be received with thanksgiving of them which believe and know the truth. 4 For every creature of God is good, and nothing to be refused, if it be received with thanksgiving: 5 For it is sanctified by the word of God and prayer.

There are many Christians who are **weak in their faith**. Who is weak in their faith? People who have convictions that really do not make a difference. They get caught up in all kinds of crusades dealing with meats, holy days, Sabbath days, clothing, etc. when it really is all about the **character, nature, and divine attributes of God**.

Romans 14:1-3 Him that is weak in the faith receive ye, but not to doubtful disputations. 2 For one believeth that he may eat all things: another, who is weak, eateth herbs. 3 Let not him that eateth despise him that eateth not; and let not him which eateth not judge him that eateth: for God hath received him. Romans 14:5-6 One man esteemeth one day above another: another esteemeth every day alike. Let every man be fully persuaded in his own mind. 6 He that regardeth the day, regardeth it unto the Lord; and he that regardeth not the day, to the Lord he doth not regard it. He that eateth, eateth to the Lord, for he giveth God thanks; and he that eateth not, to the Lord he eateth not, and giveth God thanks.

The perfect will of God is revealed to us through **Jesus Christ**. He is the brightness of God's glory, the express image of His person. If you have seen **Jesus Christ**, then you have seen the **Father**. Let us now adventure into the **third way in which faith comes**.

Romans 12:1-2 I beseech you therefore, brethren, by the mercies of God, that ye present your bodies a living sacrifice, holy, acceptable unto God, which is your reasonable service. 2 And be not conformed to this world: but be ye transformed by the renewing of your mind, that ye may prove what is that good, and acceptable, and perfect, will of God.

Audacious, Radical, Holy, Violent Faith comes by the renewing of our mind by meditating on Scripture. There must be a transformation in our thinking process: through meditation. We have to take our head and our heart and give them to God. All of who we are needs to be given over to God.

Isaiah 26:3 Thou wilt keep him in perfect peace, whose mind is stayed on thee: because he trusteth in thee.

Proverbs 3:5-6 Trust in the LORD with all thine heart; and lean not unto thine own understanding. 6 In all thy ways acknowledge him, and he shall direct thy paths.

The Scriptures declare in *Amos 3:3*: *'Can two walk together, except they be agreed?'* Therefore, if **two be not agreed together, they cannot walk together**. Faith is when we come into complete agreement with God: His Word and His will. In Romans 12:2 Paul declares, by the Spirit of God, that we are not to be conformed to this world - but transformed (**metamorphosis**). This means being changed by the renewing of our mind.

Before our mind is transformed and renewed we are like a **caterpillar**. Now, when a **caterpillar** becomes a **Butterfly** everything changes. Including the number of feet they have! And even their purpose. The number of legs, and feet, a **caterpillar** has varies according to species. There's one type of caterpillar that has sixteen legs, and sixteen feet, which, they use to hold onto anything and everything they can.

All butterflies end up with SIX legs and SIX feet. In some species, such as the monarch butterfly, the front pair of legs remains tucked up under the body most of the time. Their legs become long and slender, and something amazing happens to their feet; within their feet are now taste buds. That means whatever their feet touch - they taste. It prevents them from eating anything that is not good for them. When they were **caterpillars** they were willing to eat everything their little feet took a hold of.

Now the **Butterfly** (which came from the caterpillar) lives in a completely different world. It is no longer bound by earthly things. It no longer has feet that cling to the earth. It is free to fly above all the worries, fears, anxieties, enemies, and circumstances of life. It can see into the future and where it is going. It has overcome the law of gravitation by a superior law: the law of aerodynamics. We as believers, as we renew our minds, leave behind the law of sin and death. We enter into a new world called: **The Law of the Spirit of Life in Christ Jesus**! We need to be very picky with what we eat mentally. For whatever we place in our minds and our hearts is what we will meditate upon.

Proverbs 23:7 For as he thinketh in his heart, so is he:

Romans 8:2 For the law of the Spirit of life in Christ Jesus hath made me free from the law of sin and death.

To operate in God's Kingdom, you need to **renew your mind**. Your faith level cannot be higher than that of the **renewing of your mind**. Everything that is contradictory to the Word, the will and the divine nature of **Jesus Christ** must be dealt with. As you bring **every thought captive** to the obedience of **Christ**, your **faith**

will soar like an eagle. Listen to what James, the brother of **Jesus,** said about the renewing of the mind: *James 1:21 Wherefore lay apart all filthiness and superfluity of naughtiness, and receive with meekness the engrafted word, which is able to save your souls.*

WE CANNOT BE DEFEATED WHEN WE ARE LIVING, WALKING & MOVING IN FAITH!

What if I told you that your usefulness to God can only equal the level of faith you have in Christ! The faith I am referring to here is true faith. This is a faith that will take a hold of God (like Jacob wrestling with the Angel) and refuse to let go, until there is a wonderful transformation in your Heart and in your Mind!

There are so many Scriptures dealing with the renewal of your mind, and the meditations of your heart, that many books could easily be written on this subject. I will share with you only a small number of Scriptures that are important to this particular chapter. Then I will show you how to meditate. Here are the Scriptures:

Joshua 1:8 This book of the law shall not depart out of thy mouth; but thou shalt meditate therein day and night, that thou mayest observe to do according to all that is written therein: for then thou shalt make thy way prosperous, and then thou shalt have good success.

Psalm 1:2 But his delight is in the law of the Lord; and in his law doth he meditate day and night.

Psalm 63:6 when I remember thee upon my bed, and meditate on thee in the night watches.

Psalm 77:12 I will meditate also of all thy work, and talk of thy doings.

Psalm 119:148 Mine eyes prevent the night watches, that I might meditate in thy word.

Psalm 104:34 My meditation of him shall be sweet: I will be glad in the Lord.

Psalm 119:97 O how love I thy law! it is my meditation all the day.

Psalm 119:99 I have more understanding than all my teachers: for thy testimonies are my meditation.

1 Timothy 4:15 Meditate upon these things; give thyself wholly to them; that thy profiting may appear to all.

Psalm 39:3 My heart was hot within me, while I was musing the fire burned: then spake I with my tongue,

2 Samuel 23:2 The Spirit of the Lord spake by me, and his word was in my tongue.

What Is Meditation?

To meditate means to: **Muse**, **Ponder**, **Think Upon**, **Mutter**, **Recite**, **Talk to Yourself**. It is way more than just memorization. In the most basic form, meditation would be what we call worrying. But, it's actually the opposite of worrying! When we worry about something it is like a record stuck in a groove - it keeps on playing over and over. Have you ever had a song that just would not leave your mind? You sang it to yourself, in your mind and with your lips, because it got into your head ... and your heart. This is meditation! What we need to do is meditate upon the Word, the will and the personality of **Jesus Christ** day and night. This will bring about a wonderful transformation.

In nature, God has given us many examples that can be applied spiritually. I think one of the greatest examples of meditation is revealed to us through the process of dairy cows turning green grass into wonderful white, creamy milk.

How Do Cows Produce Milk? or we could say: How Do Believers Produce Faith?

#1 A cow only starts to produce milk once her first calf is born.

Even so, we must become impregnated by the Word of God; being born again by the Spirit and the water, in order to walk where Jesus walked.

#2 A cow only produces milk as long as she eats massive amounts of living, green grass (chewing the cud) and she needs to be milked. If any of these processes are stopped: she will stop producing milk.

The believer must keep eating the Living Word of God, chew on it, and then do it! Doing it equals the dairy cow being milked!

John 6:53-55 Then Jesus said unto them, Verily, verily, I say unto you, Except ye eat the flesh of the Son of man, and drink his blood, ye have no life in you. 54 Whoso eateth my flesh, and drinketh my blood, hath eternal life; and I will raise him up at the last day. 55 For my flesh is meat indeed, and my blood is drink indeed.

#3 Cows belong to a group of mammals called ruminants. All of these animals have **four stomach compartments** and each compartment has a specific part in digesting food. Amazingly, sheep are included in this animal group! The transformation of turning grass into milk is not instantaneous, or accomplished quickly. It takes around **Seventy hours** for a cow to turn grass into milk!

Even so is it with faith. As you begin to meditate upon the word consistently; hour after hour, day after day, faith will begin to be produced in your heart and your life. Many believers do not have this understanding. They chew a little bit of the Word, for a little bit of time, and then are disappointed when faith does not pour out of their hearts like a mighty river.

#4 Blood has a significant part in the cow producing milk. For every **2-3 cups of milk** a cow produces, more than **105 gallons** of blood must travel around her udder to deliver the nutrients and water for making milk. In total, a cow has about **12 gallons** of blood in her body, so her blood is always **on the move** (around the udder) to keep making milk.

Even so with the believer, there must be a continual moving of the Holy Spirit in our lives for us to produce faith. This is why Jesus asked if there will be any faith left on the Earth when He returns? It is because there is very little moving of the Spirit in many church gatherings today - much less in a believers everyday life. And yet in Ephesians it tells us to be filled with the Spirit, chapter 5 verse 17. It will take massive amounts of the Word and the moving of the Spirit to produce the faith that is necessary to live the same life that Jesus did!

#5 To produce milk: cows must eat a variety of grasses, clover and bulky fodder, which make them feel full. Plus, they need food rich in protein and energy. If the pasture (**pastor**) they are eating from is not providing the right kind of foods, it will cause the cow to produce dismal results. It only takes the cow to be eating one wrong type of vegetation for it to ruin its milk. And this can have dire consequences to the health of the cow … it could even die!

Even so is it with the believer. If the pastor (pasture) is not providing healthy, spiritual truths and preaching the reality of Jesus Christ, His will and His purposes; it will not produce faith that prevails and overcomes the obstacles of life.

Now let us take a look at the four stomach (digestive) compartments and their special functions:

The stomach: The heart of man, his mind, will, emotions, attitude, disposition and purpose for living could be likened unto the cows stomach.

---

1. The Rumen

When cows graze on grass they swallow the grass half-chewed and mix it with water in their first stomach (the rumen) which can hold about **13 gallons** of chewed grass. It is here that the digestive process begins. The rumen softens and breaks down the grass with stomach juices and microbes (or bacteria).

Even so with the believer, we begin to hide Scriptures within our heart. We memorize the Scriptures. This is the first process. The Holy Spirit can do very little with the Scriptures until they are memorized.

---

2. The Reticulum

In the reticulum the grass is made even softer and is formed into small wads called "cuds." Each cud is then returned to the mouth, where the cow chews it between **forty to sixty** times (which takes about one minute) and each cud is chewed for almost one hour!

Once the believer has memorized the Scripture it must be spoken (or chewed) for at least an hour. Within this time frame the Holy Spirit begins to change the Word of God from letter into spirit.

---

3. The Omasum

The chewed cud is swallowed into the third stomach "the omasum" where it is pressed to remove water and broken down further.

This is where things really begin to get interesting. Now the Word begins to be assimilated into your heart. It begins to take upon it a reality that you have never known. Furthermore, it begins to renew and transform your mind.

In Psalm 39:3 King David said: "My heart was hot within me, while I was musing the fire burned: then spake I with my tongue,"

---

4. The Abomasum

The grass then passes to the fourth stomach "the abomasum" where it is digested. The digested grass passes through the small intestine, where all the essential nutrients the cow needs to stay healthy and strong are absorbed, and some are transported to the udder.

Life is now beginning to flood the believer. Divine wisdom and strength is beginning to overtake them. The reality of Christ is exploding in their minds, their thoughts, their deeds, and their actions. Even as the milk comes forth from the udder of the cow, so now the works of the Kingdom are being produced through our lives. People are beginning to see, hear, and experience Jesus Christ in and through us!

#12 Walking Through The Fire By Meditation Of The WORD.

In 1979 we ended up being pastors at a little church in Three Springs, Pennsylvania. The church did not have very much money and the parsonage that we lived in was very old and dilapidated. There was a large porch deck over a garage area. One day my wife was walking on the deck when she broke through the flooring. Praise God she didn't get hurt! The amount of fuel oil we went through to keep it warm was ridiculous, so I decided to put a wood-burning stove in the half-basement of the parsonage.

The floor of the basement was nothing but rocks and dirt and the wood-burning stove was a long, deep, cast-iron outfit. There was an existing chimney in the basement: so I hooked the wood stove into this chimney. It was a very old system, however, and there was very little draft, which made it was extremely hard to get a good fire going. In the process of trying to keep the fire going, I would consistently, somehow, place my hands against the stove. I do not know how many blisters I got from that wood stove. It seemed as if I could not help but burn my hands! You'd think that I'd have begun to believe God for wisdom - not to burn my hands - but that's not what I did! Instead, I began to confess verses about the fire not being able to burn me.

This went on for a number of weeks, and sure enough (without fail) I would touch the stove by accident; yet I was getting burned less and less. My hand or fingers would simply turn red. One day, I once again touched the stove when it was literally glowing red (that's how hot the stove was!) Instantly my hand hurt. I put my other hand over the burnt part of my hand and commanded the pain to cease. I confessed that I would have no blister. Sure enough, the pain left and my hand was only slightly pink.

Isaiah 43:2 When thou passest through the waters, I will be with thee; and through the rivers, they shall not overflow thee: when thou walkest through the fire, thou shalt not be burned; neither shall the flame kindle upon thee.

Daniel 3:25-27 He answered and said, Lo, I see four men loose, walking in the midst of the fire, and they have no hurt; and the form of the fourth is like the Son of God. 26 Then Nebuchadnezzar came near to the mouth of the burning fiery furnace, and spake, and said, Shadrach, Meshach, and Abednego, ye servants of the most high God, come forth, and come hither. Then Shadrach, Meshach, and Abednego, came forth of the midst of the fire. 27 And the princes, governors, and captains, and the king's counsellors, being gathered together, saw these men, upon whose bodies the fire had no power, nor was an hair of their head singed, neither were their coats changed, nor the smell of fire had passed on them.

I was cooking breakfast one morning and put some cooking-oil in a cast-iron skillet. I was making eggs, bacon, and hash browns. As I was busy making breakfast, there was a knock on the door. I opened the door to one of my parishioners named Paul. Paul and I were good friends and we would spend hours together praying and witnessing. He probably was fifteen years my senior. So, I invited him into the house and we began to talk about the things of God. I had completely forgotten about the cast-iron skillet on the stove!

The next thing I knew, my wife was screaming! I went into the kitchen and saw that the oil in the skillet had exploded into fire - with flames reaching as high as the old pine wood kitchen cupboards. I knew if I did not move fast the whole house would go up in flames. The house was a firetrap waiting to happen. I was not thinking ... I yelled for Paul to open the outside door as I was running for the stove and the skillet. I scooped the red-hot skillet up into my hands, spun around, and carried it out the door. Paul was standing out of the way and my wife was watching everything as it happened. I ran outside and flipped the pan upside down on the ground.

After a while the flames went out. I was standing and looking down at the cast-iron skillet when I suddenly realized what I had done ... I looked down at my hands in complete amazement. They should have been severely burned. All that happened was that they became a little red. Not only that, but how come the flames of the burning oil did not burn me? In just a brief period of time, all the pain and the redness in my hands were completely gone.

Hebrews 11:33-34 Who through faith subdued kingdoms, wrought righteousness, obtained promises, stopped the mouths of lions, 34 Quenched the violence of fire, escaped the edge of the sword, out of weakness were made strong, waxed valiant in fight, turned to flight the armies of the aliens.

#13 Why I Canceled My FREE Health Care Policy!

I Told the Church Board to Cancel My Health Insurance Policy, which the church was paying for!

Back in 1980, my wife and I were pasturing an Assembly of God Church in Three Springs, Pennsylvania. The church automatically gave free health insurance to their pastors. I asked to have a special meeting with the board and informed the board that I wanted to save them money. They asked me how I could save them money: I told them they could cancel our health insurance policy because we did not need it. My wife and I had agreed previously that we did not need it.

To many people (Christians) this would seem preposterous and blatantly arrogant. But you see, at nineteen-years-old when I gave my heart to Christ, I had a divine Revelation of healing. I saw Christ upon the whipping post in a vision. I saw the cat o' nine tails strike His back; I saw the flesh and the blood splashing in all directions. I saw the overwhelming pain and agony upon the face of Jesus as He took those thirty-nine lashes. As I was seeing this open vision I heard the Lord say to me: "By My Stripes, You Are Healed!"

From 1975, up to the present, I have looked to God for my healing. Before this time I was always at the doctors, or laid up in a hospital bed. Pastor Mike: Have you ever taken your family to the doctors? Yes, I have, and they know that if they ask me to take them to the doctors I will - with no condemnation upon them! God will always work with us where we are at. But our whole motive should be to go deeper, higher, and wider with Christ in our walk of faith.

My wife, and my children, have been healed many times as we pray together and look to Christ for our healing. Yes ... there have been a number of times when minor operations were required on our bodies; but overall, we have lived a doctor free life. The Great Physician has been there for us. Many times when it seemed hopeless and I would cry out to Jesus all night long sometimes - even for months on end – Christ, the Great Physician, would show up and Heal my children, my wife, and myself.

I do not think it is God's will to heal me and my family. I KNOW It Is His Will! Many times, through the years, people have contacted me and wanted me to fight the fight of faith for them. Oh and how I wish I could. But it is their responsibility to take a hold of God, and not let go.

The board members at Three Springs Assembly of God agreed to my request. From the time my wife and I married (1978-present) we have not had healthcare insurance. I know the government is trying to require us to do so, but truly we would rather look to Jesus. We will obey the laws of the land, if it is required, but Christ is our Healer. It is my greatest desire to bring people into this place of freedom. Where Christ is our all in all! This is not a matter of pride. If I felt in my heart that I needed help from the medical world - because I was not where I needed to be spiritually - I would seek help. My three sons and my daughter who are now all in their 30s live in this same realm. None of them have health care insurance because they are strong in faith when it comes to their own personal healing.

The minute any one of us begins to get symptoms of sickness we immediately we lay hands upon each other and command the illness to go and our bodies to be healed. Does the healing manifest right away, all the time? The answer to that is: NO! Why? Because The Word of God Says That We Have Need of Patience! That is the time from which you pray and believe, until the manifestation of the healing. During this time we just keep on rejoicing and thanking God that it is done. Based upon the fact: By the Stripes of Jesus we are healed!

What has happened to me in the past, when I perceived that I was not where I needed to be spiritually to receive my healing, is that I would simply dig in deeper. I would once again begin to cry out to God, hide HIS Word in my heart, and go radically after Jesus. **He Has Never Failed To HEAL Us**!

Mark 11:24-25 Therefore I say unto you, What things soever ye desire, when ye pray, believe that ye receive them, and ye shall have them. And when ye stand praying, forgive, if ye have ought against any: that your Father also which is in heaven may forgive you your trespasses.

Violent Faith Comes By Prayer and Fasting

We need to understand the importance of faith. I think most believers have not really grasped the importance of **Faith**.

Hebrews 11:6 But without faith it is impossible to please him: for he that cometh to God must believe that he is, and that he is a rewarder of them that diligently seek him.

Hebrews chapter 11 is considered the **Faith Hall of Fame**. These are the saints, who by faith, fulfilled the will of God. And because they had faith that produced obedience and action; they accomplished amazing and impossible tasks. Of course, Hebrews chapter 11 is an account of the Old Testament Saints. How much greater can be accomplished now with the New Testament? Based upon better promises through the blood of **Jesus Christ**. This book is specifically written to help you enter into that realm of faith: where all things are possible. Let us now take a look at the fifth way that faith comes. Beginning with *Matthew 17:14-21:*

14 And when they were come to the multitude, there came to him a certain man, kneeling down to him, and saying, 15 Lord, have mercy on my son: for he is lunatick, and sore vexed: for ofttimes he falleth into the fire, and oft into the water. 16 And I brought him to thy disciples, and they could not cure him. 17 Then Jesus answered and said, O faithless and perverse generation, how long shall I be with you? how long shall I suffer you? bring him hither to me. 18 And Jesus rebuked the devil; and he departed out of him: and the child was cured from that very hour. 19 Then came the disciples to Jesus apart, and said, Why could not we cast him out? 20 And Jesus said unto them, Because of your unbelief: for verily I say unto you, If ye have faith as a grain of mustard seed, ye shall say unto this mountain, Remove hence to yonder place; and it shall remove; and nothing shall be impossible unto you. 21 Howbeit this kind goeth not out but by prayer and fasting.

 We need to look very carefully at the attitude of **Jesus** when it comes to unbelief. He said that His generation was faithless, which equates to being rebellious, obstinate, stubborn, and unbelieving. He asked: "how long shall I suffer you?" Unbelief is completely opposite to faith, trusting and believing. When we do not trust in God and what He has said, we are literally calling Him a liar! It is hard for us to wrap our carnal minds around this truth. The greatest offense to God is our refusal to trust and believe Him. It literally cuts us off from all that God desires to do in, through and by us.

Hebrews 6:18 That by two immutable things, in which it was impossible for God to lie, we might have a strong consolation, who have fled for refuge to lay hold upon the hope set before us:

James 1:17 Every good gift and every perfect gift is from above, and cometh down from the Father of lights, with whom is no variableness, neither shadow of turning.

Numbers 23:19 God is not a man that he should lie, neither the son of man that he should repent: hath he said, and shall he not do it? or hath he spoken, and shall he not make it good?

Jesus told His disciples that if they had faith the size of a grain of mustard seed ... ***nothing would be impossible!*** **Christ** was not exaggerating when He declared this truth. Every word He spoke was absolute, pure, unadulterated truth. We can stake our eternal and immortal souls upon His words. They asked Him: "why could not we cast him [these devils] out?" Notice that His answer was unequivocally **because of their unbelief**! Or you could say it was because they were not operating in strong faith.

Yes ... but in verse 21, did **Jesus** not say that this kind of devil only comes out by prayer and fasting? Well, I think we need to ask ourselves, was He really speaking about the devil? Or was He speaking about unbelief? One of the reasons the disciples were moving in unbelief was because of what they were hearing from the demon-possessed boy's father - about his son's condition. If you look at the other gospels you'll notice that the father of this demon-possessed boy was obsessed with the manifestations and shenanigans of the demons that were in his son. Listen very carefully! Anytime somebody brags about the devil, in whatever circumstance they find themselves in, they are not operating in faith.

In one of the other gospels **Jesus** simply asked the man: "when did this come upon your son?" **Christ** knew that somehow the door had been opened for the demons to go into this young boy. But the father began to go on in a braggadocio's manner of the manifestations of the devils. That's when **Jesus** declared they were a faithless generation! Please get it deep into your heart: **never brag about the devil**, your problems, or any evil thing. Notice, I'm not telling you to ignore them - I'm simply saying do not boast or brag about them.

Ephesians 5:11-13 And have no fellowship with the unfruitful works of darkness, but rather reprove them. 12 For it is a shame even to speak of those things which are done of them in secret.

13 But all things that are reproved are made manifest by the light: for whatsoever doth make manifest is light.

The spirit of unbelief is so deep in every one of us that it will take Prayer and Fasting for it to come out.

Now let's break down those two words:

#1 Prayer

When I talk about prayer, I'm not referring to some type of religious ceremony. Let us get right to the nitty-gritty here. I'm talking about divine and intimate fellowship with the **Father, Son** and **Holy Ghost**. It is that invisible umbilical cord connected to God. What is it that we pray? We pray the known will and purposes of the **Father**! We pray the Word of God within biblical context.

1 Thessalonians 5:17 Pray without ceasing.

2 Timothy 1:3 I thank God, whom I serve from my forefathers with pure conscience, that without ceasing I have remembrance of thee in my prayers night and day;

Philippians 4:6 Be careful for nothing; but in every thing by prayer and supplication with thanksgiving let your requests be made known unto God.

Many people erroneously teach that there is power in prayer; but in truth there isn't. The power is not in the prayer itself and many pray to false deities, idols, and religions. The power is not in the prayer but in the One we are praying to. And He is the One that has all power, authority and dominion. As we are speaking to God and we pray His Will and His Word, faith will begin to rise in our heart. When we pray, the Spirit of the Lord will begin to fall upon us like rain. And even as rain causes the seed to bud, and to bring forth fruit, so our faith will begin to grow. The more intimate we grow with God, the greater our faith will become. Now let's take a look at fasting.

#2 Fasting

Dealing with the subject of fasting could be a book within itself. Many have taught mystical things about this subject. There are books that attribute things to fasting which the Scriptures do not teach. In this particular context we are dealing with the subject of denying our flesh. I am talking about driving out unbelief. We must say **NO** to our flesh - by faith. Fasting does not only deal with the subject of food, but also desires and actions that are against the will of God. Denying our flesh is actually an act of faith - even as prayer is an act of faith in **Christ**. **Faith** is like the physical muscles in your body. If you do not use them: they begin to shrivel up and become useless. But if you will exercise them on a daily basis, they will become strong and powerful. As we exercise our faith by prayer and fasting, it will become strong and solid in **Christ**.

Matthew 16:24 Then said Jesus unto his disciples, If any man will come after me, let him deny himself, and take up his cross, and follow me.

Mark 8:34 And when he had called the people unto him with his disciples also, he said unto them, Whosoever will come after me, let him deny himself, and take up his cross, and follow me.

Titus 2:12 Teaching us that, denying ungodliness and worldly lusts, we should live soberly, righteously, and godly, in this present world;

Let us delve a little bit deeper into the subject of unbelief by looking at what Paul declared in the book of Romans. It is important that we recognize that unbelief must not be allowed to live in our lives. It is the seed of unbelief that is the root cause of all of man's wickedness and sin.

Romans 11:19-23 Thou wilt say then, The branches were broken off, that I might be grafted in. 20 Well; because of <u>unbelief</u> they were broken off, and thou standest by <u>faith</u>. Be not highminded, but fear: 21 For if God spared not the natural branches, take heed lest he also spare not thee. 22 Behold therefore the goodness and severity of God: on them which fell, severity; but toward thee, goodness, if thou continue in his goodness: otherwise thou also shalt be cut off. 23 And they also, if they abide not still in <u>unbelief,</u> shall be grafted in: for God is able to graft them in again.

Unbelief is extremely demonic and diabolical.

Unbelief says: I do not have to obey God. Unbelief is literally the voice of the devil speaking to all of us, accusing God, and making Him a liar. But let God be true and everything else a lie. Did you know that the Bible says whatever is not of faith is sin! The reason the **Father** said: **"This Is My Son in Whom I Am Well Pleased"** is because Jesus had no unbelief operating in His mind or heart. He gave absolutely no place to the devil. This same **Jesus** is in us. We need to put our faith and confidence in Him by allowing Him to rise up within us and to overcome every work of unbelief.

*Faith is the voice of God! *Unbelief is the voice of the devil!

Luke 4:1-2 & 14-15 And Jesus being full of the Holy Ghost returned from Jordan, and was led by the Spirit into the wilderness, 2 Being forty days tempted of the devil. And in those days he did eat nothing: and when they were ended, he afterward hungered..................14 And Jesus returned in the power of the Spirit into Galilee: and there went out a fame of him through all the region round about. 15 And he taught in their synagogues, being glorified of all.

If we closely examine Luke chapter 4, we discover that **Jesus** was deep in prayer during His whole time of testing. He was in constant communion with His Heavenly **Father**. During these forty days He denied His flesh any earthly food. And in verse 14 it says He returned in the Power of the Spirit. When people are full of faith they will be full of Power and the Holy Ghost. I'm not saying that you have to go forty days without natural food: **To have this type of faith there must be continual communion with God and a denial of your flesh.**

There must be a lifestyle of self-denial. We must deny ourselves from anything that is displeasing to the Heavenly **Father**. We must also deny ourselves anything that would get between us and God's divine plan for our lives. After **Jesus** came out of the wilderness, by passing the test and denying the flesh, He was filled with the Power of the Spirit and He set the captives free. From then on, miracles began to flow like a mighty river out of His innermost being. Now, you might say: "It was the Holy Ghost" and you would be absolutely correct. The Holy Ghost uses vessels that have been prepared for the Master's use. The vessels that are full of faith in **Christ**.

Acts 6:8 And Stephen, full of faith and power, did great wonders and miracles among the people.

Acts 11:24 For he was a good man, and full of the Holy Ghost and of faith: and much people was added unto the Lord.

God moved upon those within the early church to pray and fast. Prayer and fasting does not change the mind or the heart of God, but it brings us into a place of harmony with God. **It is a place of Faith and Power.**

Acts 10:30 And Cornelius said, Four days ago I was fasting until this hour; and at the ninth hour I prayed in my house, and, behold, a man stood before me in bright clothing,

Acts 13:2-3 As they ministered to the Lord, and fasted, the Holy Ghost said, Separate me Barnabas and Saul for the work whereunto I have called them. 3 And when they had fasted and prayed, and laid their hands on them, they sent them away.

Acts 14:23 And when they had ordained them elders in every church, and had prayed with fasting, they commended them to the Lord, on whom they believed.

Let's look at one more example of the life of **Jesus,** in the Gospel of Luke chapter 22. **Jesus** is our supreme example of walking, living, moving and operating in faith:

Luke 22:39-46 And he came out, and went, as he was wont, to the mount of Olives; and his disciples also followed him. 40 And when he was at the place, he said unto them, Pray that ye enter not into temptation. 41 And he was withdrawn from them about a stone's cast, and kneeled down, and prayed, 42 Saying, Father, if thou be willing, remove this cup from me: nevertheless not my will, but thine, be done. 43 And there appeared an angel unto him from heaven, strengthening him. 44 And being in an agony he prayed more earnestly: and his sweat was as it were great drops of blood falling down to the ground. 45 And when he rose up from prayer, and was come to his disciples, he found them sleeping for sorrow, 46 And said unto them, Why sleep ye? rise and pray, lest ye enter into temptation.

Jesus told His disciples that they must pray (have communion with the **Father**) lest they enter into temptation. First John chapter 5 says that it is faith in **Christ** that overcomes the world!

Prayer and fasting is a way God has provided for faith; to come, grow, and mature!

Jesus, in the time of His greatest test and trial, prayed without ceasing. When He said, not my will be done, but yours **Father**. This was self-denial; the fasting of that which was not God's will: but the **Father**'s will be done. Notice the Scripture says an angel came to strengthen Him. Why? Because He was operating in pure, holy faith. Faith is an invisible magnet that will draw God to you. The angelic world will come rushing to a man or woman moving in this type of faith. It's like the attraction of a flower to a honeybee. You want God to show up in your life?

Then you need to begin to move in this realm of faith. How can this be accomplished? **By Prayer and Fasting.**

#14 My Son Healed Of An Incurable Affliction (1987)

When my son, Daniel, was little, he loved to put things in his mouth. While he was in the back seat of my sister's car he found a can of WD-40. He was always very inquisitive and nosy (and still is - to this day!) So, when he discovered the can of chemicals, his curiosity, and natural desire to put things in his mouth, got the better of him. He sucked on the end of the can and the cap popped off! Not only did he ingest the WD-40 but it also leaked all over him. By the time we realized what had happened, he was having a hard time breathing. I prayed over him, but he didn't seem to be getting any better. This chemical is not something to mess with!

Kathleen and I got someone to watch Michael while we took Daniel to our doctor straightaway. We informed the doctor what had happened and he strongly suggested x-rays, so we gave our approval. Lung problems had been a generational curse in my family and I did not want Daniel to go through the same misery that I, and other members of my family, had gone through. My mother had died from medication related to her lung problems.

When the x-rays came back, the doctor's prognosis was not very encouraging. He showed us the x-rays and the chemicals in Daniel's body were very dangerous and were lining his lungs. Our doctor informed us that there was nothing anybody could do for Daniel. He also told us that Daniel would always have breathing problems because of the chemicals in his lungs. We thanked the doctor for his help, paid the medical bill, and left his office. From then on it was a fight for Daniel's life.

Many times, late at night, I would hear Daniel struggling to breathe. I would get up immediately, take him into my arms and pray over him. I kept on commanding the chemicals to come out of Daniel's lungs in the name of Jesus Christ of Nazareth. I prayed with him in the midst of it - thanking and praising God that he was healed. I stayed with Daniel until his breathing was normal, and then I would put him back to bed. This went on for many months. I began to notice that after each episode it would happen less and less often. It has been over twenty-years since Daniel has had an attack. Thank God, he is completely healed!

Matthew 24:13-14 But he that shall endure unto the end, the same shall be saved. 14 And this gospel of the kingdom shall be preached in all the world for a witness unto all nations; and then shall the end come.

CHAPTER FIVE

By FAITH I Refused to Take A Wealthy Man's Money! (1984)

If we are going to have Violent, Audacious, Overcoming Faith, then we have to listen very carefully to the Voice of God!

One of the most important aspects of having a **Violent Faith** that overcomes, is to move in a **faith that works by love!** Our faith needs to overcome the tendency of being Self-Loving, Self-Serving, Self-Seeking, and Self Pleasing. We must come to a place where we are not taking advantage of people in any way, form, or fashion.

Galatians 5:6 For in Jesus Christ neither circumcision availeth any thing, nor uncircumcision; but faith which worketh by love.

#15 Give Your Wealth To Your Family, And Not To Us, I Told Him!

Some years ago, there was a very wealthy and famously wicked man in our community. He was the talk of the town! I won't be too descriptive about who he was because this is not a negative story. This particular wealthy, and legendary, man became extremely sick and went to see his doctor. He discovered that he had incurable cancer. One of our elders met him at some event and He shared Christ with him. Consequently, this man, sincerely, and with all true intents, gave his heart to Jesus Christ.

As a result of his conversion, he began to attend the church I pastored. Because of my wild upbringing, and rough background I could really relate to him. It wasn't too long before we were not just a pastor and a parishioner, but friends. Of course, we laid hands on him and believed God for complete healing from the cancer. Well, Praise God! Sure enough, the cancer went into remission! Up to that point, the medical world had told him there was no hope … but the cancer was going into remission! They convinced him to take chemo and radiation treatment. Within the last forty years, I have seen this happen more times than I want to think about.

I have watched the medical world tell people there is no hope but, all of a sudden, when the cancer begins to go into remission they jump on the bandwagon. Convincing people that now they should take their treatments - even though they could not help them before. Don't misunderstand me, I am not on a crusade against the medical world. It's just that it saddens my heart, because of all the people I have watched die from radiation and chemo.

It was no different for this precious brother. I watched as he went from a fairly heavyset man, to skin and bones. He was sent home to die with hospice care. I would usually visit him two to three times a week, to pray and encourage him. One day, I received a phone call from his brother, asking if I could go over to talk. When I arrived at his house he informed me that he was tired of the fight. That he wanted to go home, to be with Jesus. I told him I completely understood, and that we would all miss him.

Then he informed me of the reason he had asked me to visit him. He told me that he had much wealth, and he was being tormented. He wanted to give his money to our church, but, he felt in his heart he had done wrong to his children all their lives. And, even though they were now grown adults, he felt that he should bless his children with the wealth he'd leave behind. He asked me, with all sincerity: "Pastor, what should I do?" In the natural, the church I was pastoring desperately needed money, but who was I to take advantage of this precious brother? I looked into his tear-filled eyes, and informed him to obey God: "If the Lord is telling you to give your wealth to your children, then do it!" He sincerely thanked me. I prayed with him, tears flowing down my face, knowing that I was going to miss him. I left his house knowing that would be the last time I saw him alive, on this side of heaven.

He went home to be with the Lord that night. His children knew that he had been attending our church on a very regular basis. Every time I saw his children, they seemed to be antagonistic towards me. I knew, in my heart, that they thought I was after their father's money. It must have been in his instructions for me to do his funeral because I received a phone call from the funeral director asking if I would do the service. Of course, I said that I would.

On that day, when I walked into the funeral home, I could see many eyes were on me. I can tell you now, they were not eyes filled with love and appreciation for the time I had spent with their father. As far as I understand it, his last will, and last testament, were not read until after the funeral. For all they knew, because I had become very close to their father, he would probably leave a sizable amount of his wealth to our church. Of course, they found out after the service, this was not the case.

I am not sharing this story to make it look like I am spiritual. Yes ... in the natural, we could have really used the money. But that is not the issue. What did God want this man to do? That is the question. I believe every born-again believer needs to hear from heaven, and not be manipulated by those of us who are called to be spiritual leaders! The Scriptures declare that we are not to be many masters; knowing that we shall receive the greater condemnation. God forbid that I would stand before the Lord, and give an account of using and manipulating people! I do not believe He would be very pleased with that!

#16 Charity's Miracle (1985)

Back in 1985, we knew a wonderful couple that were very active in our church. This brother actually went to the Philippines with me on a number of occasions. His profession was that he hung and finished drywall, in which he was extremely gifted and worked very fast. Actually, he has done quite a number of jobs for the church, including doing all our drywall when we put up our new facility. One day, while he was at work, his daughter, Charity, became congested and was having difficulty breathing. His wife, not knowing what to do because it seemed like it was pretty bad, ran Charity to the nearest Emergency Room. Now, that is when their nightmare really began! The medical staff immediately wanted to admit Charity to the hospital. Well, instead of getting better … she got worse. Charity's parents wanted to take her home, and see what they could do, but the hospital would not allow them to. The hospital basically decided to ship her off to Hershey Medical Centre.

My wife and I made an emergency trip down to see Charity. She was getting worse. Charity was (I think) at this time, probably less than ten-years-old. When I walked into her hospital room, I personally became extremely upset. Here they had her, in a hospital bed, directly underneath an air conditioning vent. The cold air was being pumped down on top of her, and she was wearing a very thin nightgown. Not only this, but because she wanted to go home with her parents, the medical staff had strapped her to the bed: like she was some kind of criminal.

So here poor little Charity is strapped to the bed with a very thin nightgown, the air conditioning is being pumped over the top of her, and she is shivering and getting worse every moment. It upset me so much, that I did mention something to one of the medical personnel - but they simply ignored me. We prayed for her, with heavy hearts, knowing that if God did not intervene they would literally kill her. There is nobody who could be strapped to a bed, on their back, with cold air-conditioning being dumped on them twenty-four hours a day and not end up with pneumonia. That is exactly what happened to Charity. Not just pneumonia, but double pneumonia. Both of her lungs filled with pneumonia and fluid.

We kept in constant contact with her parents about their little girl. The hospital was now calling every shot when it came to what they were going to do with her. They actually ended cutting open both of her lungs to scrape out the congestion, and the parts of the lungs that had died.

Right after this operation, her father came into my office. They had been saving up money in order to build a house and he informed me that he had heard from heaven. He was taking a step of faith by giving the money to the church - all the money they had saved up for building a new house. He said he needed a miracle for their little girl, and this was their seed of faith. At that moment, I actually tried to talk him out of giving this money. I told him that he could not buy a miracle from God. I said this to him very gently because I knew they were fighting for their daughter's life, and they were having to deal with the medical world: that was literally killing their little girl before their very eyes. He told me that he and his wife had prayed, and that they had definitely heard from heaven about this financial gift that they needed to make to the church. You see, we also needed a miracle. If I did not have $50,000 in just a couple of weeks ... I was going to jail. That's another story.

What could I do but tell him that if he had heard from heaven, we would accept his gift. We held hands and prayed together, believing God to divinely intervene for their little girl, Charity. He left the office believing that they had obeyed God and that somehow, God was going to divinely intervene.

Now remember, they had tried over and over to get Charity out of the hands of the medical world. It is not because they did not believe in medicine, or medical help, but they saw the medical world killing their little girl. If you do not believe that the medical world kills a lot of people, you are simply ignorant, or you have chosen to ignore the facts. They had basically given to this couple a death sentence for their daughter. We all, together, especially her parents, took a hold of God for a miracle.

Three days later I received an incredible phone call from Charity's father. He told me that his daughter was home from the hospital. In spite of everything the medical world had done to their little girl, God had instantly, and completely, healed her lungs! Praise God for answered prayer, and obedience! This miracle was not bought by a financial gift, but the fact that they had literally sacrificed the down payment they needed to build their dream house. In their hearts they were saying to God: "Father, we do not care about that house, all we care about is our little girl." God had supernaturally heard their plea and rescued their daughter from certain death.

It is approximately thirty years later now, and that little girl, Charity, has grown up to become a mother of five of her own precious children. If you ask her mom and dad, was it worth the sacrifice? They would answer with a resounding "Yes!" A million times over!

I have had dealings with the medical world - even before I was born again. After I was born again, a part of my PhD training was through a local hospital, in which they had an accredited program. I know a lot of people think highly of the medical world, but I am sorry to say I have seen too much on the other side.

Back in the early 80s, one of the head nurses for a local hospital was the wife of one of my elders. She would tell me stories that were unbelievable: of things she saw the doctors do. She was literally tormented, even though she was the head nurse for surgery. The brother-in-law of my youth pastor's wife, was a doctor, and she could not believe the things that he would say about his patients - and the amount of money he was hauling in.

In sharing this story, I am not at all trying to create animosity towards the medical world. I realize there are a lot of sincere people in the medical profession. I also realize that there are a lot of people who would be dead without medical help. On the other side of the equation, I personally know a lot of people who would still be alive if they had not believed everything they were told by the medical world.

#17 Building A Million-Dollar Facility With No Money By Faith

While I was in Great Britain, the elders of the church in Gettysburg, had made a deposit on ten-acres of land. I was twenty-nine years old at the time this happened. Now, this property was located seven miles west of Gettysburg, on Route 30. When I got back from Great Britain, they showed me the property they had placed money on. The farmer had given us a tremendous deal on this particular acreage. It was not long afterwards, however, that our church went through a terrible split. It always seems that at the worst possible moment, when things look the bleakest, God has me take a gigantic step of faith.

As I was in prayer one day, the Lord spoke to my heart to build a church that would seat eight-hundred people. The key to this miracle, is that I had heard the voice of God. It is not something that I simply grabbed out of nothingness, and decided to do myself. Now, at this time, the size of our congregation was only about seventy people. On top of this, we had no money! I knew the members of our congregation pretty well, and as far as I could tell, none of them were wealthy. When the Lord quickened my heart, I immediately acted upon on what He spoke to me. I checked into local construction companies: just to put up the exterior steel building, and pour the concrete floor, would cost more than $800,000. I knew in my heart that this was not the way to go.

There was a man in our congregation who represented a steel building company from South Dakota. We began to coordinate with his company for the purchase of the steel we needed. They provided us with all the blueprints that were necessary for the foundation. I located an architectural company in Hanover, Pennsylvania, that was willing to work with us. I drew up a rough, simple schematic of what we were looking for. With that drawing, they were able to provide for us the simplest blueprint possible, which would be approved by the state of Pennsylvania. We went through the proper process to get the right building permits from local, county, and state authorities. We had everything in hand to start the project. We had done everything we could do!

Now what? We had no money!

As I was in prayer, the Spirit of God quickened my heart to simply step out in faith and do it. There was a man in our church, Richard, who owned a backhoe. I approached Richard about what I wanted to do and he said: "Let's do it!" We went out to the property and staked out where the footers and foundations were going to be. Then he brought his son, from Maryland, to dig the footers. We ended up with a 100 x 150 foot ditch. We prayed every step of the way. As the Spirit of the Lord quickened me, I ordered the building materials.

On the day we were to lay the blocks that the metal building would sit on, it was pouring down rain. The men of the congregation wanted to cancel the Saturday work party. However, I told them that God was going to make it possible for us to lay the blocks on that day. As we were on the building site, we cried out to the Lord, and immediately the rain stopped and the sun came out! By the end of that day 500 feet of block had been laid.

2 Samuel 7:27-28 For thou, O LORD of hosts, God of Israel, hast revealed to thy servant, saying, I will build thee an house: therefore hath thy servant found in his heart to pray this prayer unto thee. 28 And now, O Lord GOD, thou art that God, and thy words be true, and thou hast promised this goodness unto thy servant:

#18 My Life On The Line (1985)

The company providing the steel for our building called from South Dakota, telling us that the steel building was almost ready to be shipped. They said they could ship it: cash on delivery. When the building arrived I would have to give them approximately **$49,000**. At the time, we only had **$1,000** in our building account - with no other means of finances. The representative from the steel company also informed us they could store the building for about $1,200 a month, or they could ship it out within six to eight weeks.

As I was listening to the man over the phone, I heard the Spirit of the Lord say to me: *"Tell them to send it!"* I became very still before the Lord, because I wanted to make sure that I had heard Him correctly. The Spirit spoke to me again: *"Tell them to send it!"* I told the man from the steel company to go ahead and send the building! He told me that would be fine and they would prepare it to be sent. He also informed me that I'd better be aware that if the building arrived, and I did not have the money, I would be breaking interstate laws (I believe he said there were five of them) and I would be going to jail: because I was the one who gave the approval for the building to be shipped! I got very quiet before the Lord and asked Him again, *"What I should do?"* The Spirit, once again, confirmed and quickened in my heart, to have them send it. So, once again, I told the representative to go ahead and send it. He gave me another warning.

The **Gift Of Faith** was operating in my heart. I knew that it was done. After I got off the phone, a desire came into my heart to give away the **$1,000** in our building account. I was not trying to bribe God to do something for us. The **$1,000** we had was not going to do a thing for us, so why not give it away - out of faith? We took that thousand dollars and divided it up into ten different checks, sending it to ten different ministries. That Sunday, I went before the congregation and told them this story. I told them the steel was coming, and if they wanted to, they could get involved. I also told them we had invested **$1,000** into ten other ministries. I did inform the congregation that if I was missing God, in this regards, I was going to have a prison ministry. I had put my life on the line ...

Amazingly, I had no fear or anxiety whatsoever during the six weeks leading up to the steel arriving. Without a shadow of a doubt, I knew the money would be there. The finances began to trickle in. To this day, I do not remember where it all came from. I did not beg, plead, or call anybody for money. I received a phone call approximately six weeks later from the representative of the steel company. They told me that they were loading the steel up on their big trucks, and asked, was I ready to receive it? At that point we were still extremely short of the finances we needed. I told them to go ahead and send it. Within three days the truck pulled onto our property.

I met the truck driver at the construction site and he handed me the paperwork. There were certain documents which I had to fill out. I started filling out the paperwork, knowing that I was still **$15,000** short of the **$49,000** that I had to pay them in just a few short moments. As I was signing the papers, one of the men from our church pulled into the parking lot. He drove his car right up to me with his window rolled down. I could see that there was something in his right hand; he handed a check to me for **$15,000**! Thank you Jesus!

I would just like to take a moment and tell you that the people in this story, who gave of their finances, were operating in a higher level of faith than I was. That may sound strange ... but it's not. We're always exalting those who believe for the money. But what about the ones who make these sacrifices to give what they have? I have been on both sides of this equation, more times than I can count. I have both given - until it hurt - and gladly received, with unspeakable joy.

#19 Supernatural Education By Faith

We had approximately thirty volunteer men assembled, to help put the steel of the building up. Men who did not attend our church came to help us. The majority were not construction workers in any fashion of the word. The Lord had put in our hearts to use volunteers to get the job done. The man we had gone through, to purchase the steel building, was to oversee this work, and was there with us. He had been consistent all the time. He helped us do the footers and concrete piers, and he did excellent quality work. The large crane we needed to put all the steel up was on the property, with its operator. I think the cost of the crane and the operator was over $150 an hour. The big machine was idling and waiting to go to work. Everyone was standing there waiting to work.

We all bombarded the leader with questions and asked for directions. He had the blueprints in his hands, and every time he went to look at them someone would approach him. The pressure on him was overwhelming. It was easy to see that he was getting extremely frustrated. From what I understand, he had not put up a building like this before, and if he had it was many years ago. More and more people kept tugging on him. Next thing I knew, one of the brothers from the church said: "Pastor Mike! There goes so and so!" I looked to see where he was pointing. Sure enough, there was the leader, going down the road in his automobile. I did not hear from him, or see him again, for quite a number of years.

At the time of construction, it seemed as if this was a satanic attack. Actually, I can now say what Joseph said, that although this situation seemed as if it was meant for evil: God meant it for good. The Lord was stretching our faith. There I was, standing in front of all of the volunteer men, who were waiting to go to work. The steel was lying on the ground and the crane was idling. I can still remember walking away from everybody, looking up to heaven, and crying out to God. I said: *"Lord, please show me how to put this building up. I had never even built a doghouse, let alone a large steel commercial building!"*

At that moment, it was as if an invisible blanket came down upon me. Wisdom entered into my heart and I knew instantly what to do: moment by moment. I grabbed the blueprints, walked towards the crane operator, and began to tell him where to put the steel. The building began to go up! Through the process, we lost volunteers and gained volunteers. The Lord began to send us skilled labor. Not much of it … but just enough!

> *Psalm 127:1 Except the LORD build the house, they labour in vain that build it: except the LORD keep the city, the watchman waketh but in vain.*

One night as I was sleeping soundly I heard the audible voice of God - as clear as a bell ringing out on a cold winter night.

This is what I heard Him say: **"The Violent Take It by Force!"** I woke straight up from my deep sleep. I was instantly fully awake and aware of God's presence.

This particular Scripture comes from *Matthew 11:12: And from the days of John the Baptist until now the kingdom of heaven suffereth violence, and the violent take it by force.*

There is a similar Scripture discovered in *Luke 16:16: The law and the prophets were until John: since that time the kingdom of God is preached, and every man presseth into it.*

Adam Clarke Commentary on Luke 16:16: The law and the prophets were until John - The law and the prophets continued to be the sole teachers till John came, who first began to proclaim the glad tidings of the kingdom of God: and now, he who wishes to be made a partaker of the blessings of that kingdom must rush speedily into it; as there will be but a short time before an utter destruction shall fall upon this ungodly race. They who wish to be saved must imitate those who take a city by storm - rush into it, without delay, as the Romans are about to do into Jerusalem. See also on Matthew 11:12.

This is pertaining to the **Violence of biblical True Faith**. As you look at the Old Testament you will see this type of faith demonstrated many times.

I challenge you to read **Hebrews 11** to get a clearer understanding of what it truly means to believe God - in spite of the circumstances.

{Faith is receiving from God, that which the heart knows to be the will of God, because you know it is the plan of God.}

And you do not allow feelings, circumstances, thoughts, emotions, or the devil, or demons, to stop you from receiving what Christ has purchased for you, in His sufferings and in His agonies.

Take Your Healing!

In this book, I share almost thirty true stories of how I had to **Fight, Persevere And Trust God For My Healing**! Yes, in every situation He made me whole! Many of these healings were not instantaneous, but it really did not matter.

For I knew, that I knew, that I knew, that God cannot lie. I've never questioned whether it was God's will to heal me.
The reason for this, is that I have read the Gospels of Matthew, Mark, Luke, and John, for myself. I did not need another minister to tell me any different. **Jesus Healed Them All!!!**

Do not allow the devil, circumstances, or any other situation, to Rob you of what Jesus did when He received those thirty-nine lashes upon His precious back. In the Name of Jesus Christ of Nazareth I Command You to Be Healed!!!

2 Corinthians 10:4-5 (For the weapons of our warfare are not carnal, but mighty through God to the pulling down of strong holds;)5 Casting down imaginations, and every high thing that exalteth itself against the knowledge of God, and bringing into captivity every thought to the obedience of Christ;

Joshua 1:8-9 This book of the law shall not depart out of thy mouth; but thou shalt meditate therein day and night, that thou mayest observe to do according to all that is written therein: for then thou shalt make thy way prosperous, and then thou shalt have good success. 9 Have not I commanded thee? Be strong and of a good courage; be not afraid, neither be thou dismayed: for the LORD thy God is with thee whithersoever thou goest .

Psalm 39:3 My heart was hot within me, while I was musing the fire burned: then spake I with my tongue,

Jeremiah 20:9 Then I said, I will not make mention of him, nor speak any more in his name. But his word was in mine heart as a burning fire shut up in my bones, and I was weary with forbearing, and I could not stay.

#21 It Took This Man More Faith To Give His Money Than It Did For Me To Receive It.

Lack of Faith and Not of Money

I was walking the floor of our sanctuary one afternoon, crying out to God concerning the finances of the church. We had some overwhelming financial needs that were weighing heavily upon my heart. At the time we had twenty-one people working for the church. Of course, we had vehicles, insurance, electricity and utility bills. Plus, we were on seven TV stations, cable stations and satellite broadcasting. As I was letting my needs be known, God said to me: *"Your problem is not money or lack of finances. Your problem is a lack of faith! You do not need more money. You need more faith in Me!"*

I took this to heart, and asked God to forgive me for complaining and whining. Just a couple of days after that, I was sitting in my office, with approximately $24,000 worth of bills in front of me. I piled all the bills in one spot, laid my hands upon the needs, and confessed every bill paid - according to God's riches in glory.

As I was praying, there was a knock on my door. I told the person who was knocking to come on in. One of the men of the church came into my office. He was a very quiet man, and we had never really spoken very much to each other. He seemed to be just a very nice, everyday kind of person. Out of the blue, he asked me: "Pastor, how much money do you need to bring all the bills up to date?" I said: "You mean to bring the bills current?" He responded, "Yes. To pay the bills up to date."

He pulled out a blank check, and began to write on it. The thought entered my mind that he was going to make a small contribution towards the bills. I told him it would take $24,000 to bring the bills up to date. He handed me a check and I thanked him for it. Then I took a peek at it. I looked up at him … and back down to the check again. He had handed me a check for $24,000! In a thousand years, I would never have guessed that this quiet man, who seemed to have no money, would have that kind of wealth available.

It took this man more faith to give that money than it did for me to receive it.

Thank God for obedient people that are willing to do what God says, no matter what it costs them. Many times, it seems to me, that we as ministers boast and brag about how we believe God for money, and yet never recognize that it took a lot more faith for the person who gave the finances, then those of us who have believed for them.

#22 How I was Healed of A Strangulated Hernia!
(1988) *I would **SHOVE** my intestines back into where they belonged: with my fingers.

Day after day, we were putting up the steel of our church in 1975. We only had the use of a crane for a couple of days during its construction. We had the crane handle all of the heaviest beams. The rest of the steel had to be carried, and placed into position, by hand. I'm not a very large man, I only weighed about 140 pounds at the time, and I was pulling and tugging, walking on steel beams, and balancing precariously with large steel beams over my shoulder; and being carried up against my gut.

One day, as I was trying to put a heavy beam into place, I felt something rip in my lower abdomen. Later that same day I noticed I had a large bulge: I had torn loose some stomach muscles. I had a hernia! I did not tell anyone. I found a quiet place and cried out to God. I laid my hands over the hernia and commanded it to go in the name of Jesus Christ of Nazareth. I went back to work - because the building had to be put up! Every day I kept on lifting heavy steel. The hernia did not go away, so I kept looking to God, trusting, and believing. The only one who became aware of the hernia was my wife. Honestly, I do not even remember telling her.

Why would I not tell anyone? It wasn't because I was afraid that people would have a poor opinion of me because I wasn't getting healed. I have never worried in the least about people thinking I did not have faith. **Faith is the substance that is or is not**. You can fake faith – but, then it's not faith. The Bible says if any man has faith, let him have it to himself. In my heart there was nothing I needed to prove. You see, my confidence is in **Jesus Christ**, the **Heavenly Father**, and the **Holy Ghost**! If I have to go to the doctor, or use medication, it's nobody's business.

For over two years the hernia remained with me. The problem was that I really was not aggressively dealing with it, but had gone into a state of passivity. I knew in my heart that it was time to deal with this monkey on my back. I began to speak to the hernia aggressively - telling it that it was gone! And I commanded my stomach lining to be made whole.

The only problem was that the hernia had now gotten to the place of being almost strangulated. It was quickened in my heart that I was going to have to get more aggressive with the hernia. So, I would take my right hand, and put my fingers against this hernia. Then I would **SHOVE** it back in where it belonged. As I **SHOVED** this hernia, I would be speaking to it: **In the name of Jesus be healed**! I commanded my **intestines** to stay where they belonged as I shoved upwards.

"Strangulated hernia: This is an irreducible hernia in which the entrapped intestine has its blood supply cut off. Pain is always present, followed quickly by tenderness and sometimes symptoms of bowel obstruction (nausea and vomiting). The affected person may appear ill with or without fever."

But … Pastor Mike: Did you not know that you could die if this hernia got strangulated? YES! I knew this, but I also knew within my heart that **By the Stripes of Jesus I Am Healed!**

I cannot tell you how many times, through the next two weeks, I kept SHOVING my intestines back up into my body with my fingertips. I would speak to it as Jesus told us to speak to the mountain. I told my stomach lining that it was healed. I told my **intestines** that they were healed and my body is the temple of the Holy Ghost, and they had no right to be giving me any problems.

One Typical Night I Went To Bed And Got Up The Next Morning To A Miracle: The Hernia Was Completely Gone!! Praise God! That was almost Thirty years ago. It has never come back.

Genesis 22:2-3 And he said, Take now thy son, thine only son Isaac, whom thou lovest, and get thee into the land of Moriah; and offer him there for a burnt offering upon one of the mountains which I will tell thee of. 3 And Abraham rose up early in the morning, and saddled his ass, and took two of his young men with him, and Isaac his son, and clave the wood for the burnt offering, and rose up, and went unto the place of which God had told him.

CHAPTER SIX

#23 Violent Faith Will Embrace The Sufferings Of Christ.

I heard a very interesting story from another minister of the gospel. Supposedly (if I have the story correct) he was in China, ministering. At the end of his service, he was having a conversation with another Chinese believer. They were talking about the sufferings, persecutions, and afflictions that were taking place in China, against the body of Christ. This particular man said he knew of a situation where the government had arrested a pastor. The pastor was taken to prison for quite a long time.

When the pastor was in prison, they began to torture him, afflict him, and do terrible things to him in order that he would renounce his faith. But, thank God, he never did. I do not know how long this went on before he was finally released, but it was implied that it was for quite a while. When he was finally let go, he eventually made it back to the church he had pastored. He stood before his congregation and shared with them his testimony: how God had preserved him and kept him - that he had not denied the faith. He also shared, in detail, all of the terrible things that had happened to him while he was in prison. All of the sufferings, tortures and pains he had endured for Jesus Christ. That day, the entire congregation, all believers, broke out in weeping and crying.

When the Chinese believer had finished telling his story, a visiting American minister said: "They must have really loved their pastor." The Chinese believer looked at him oddly and he asked: "What do you mean?" The American minister replied: "The way they were weeping and wailing, and crying for him." **The Chinese believer replied: "Oh! No! You have it all wrong! You completely misunderstand!** They were not crying because the pastor was tortured. They were weeping and crying because they felt there was something wrong with them, in the fact that they had not been arrested themselves, and tortured for Christ! They were literally jealous of their pastor for being so blessed in being tortured for Christ."

Acts 5:41 And they departed from the presence of the council, rejoicing that they were counted worthy to suffer shame for his name.

1 Peter 4:13-16 But rejoice, inasmuch as ye are partakers of Christ's sufferings; that, when his glory shall be revealed, ye may be glad also with exceeding joy. 14 If ye be reproached for the name of Christ, happy are ye; for the spirit of glory and of God resteth upon you: on their part he is evil spoken of, but on your part he is glorified. 15 But let none of you suffer as a murderer, or as a thief, or as an evildoer, or as a busybody in other men's matters. 16 Yet if any man suffer as a Christian, let him not be ashamed; but let him glorify God on this behalf.

We, as Western believers, seem to have no concept of what it really means to be God's people. I have heard from very reliable sources that the believers in China really feel sad for us. They literally pray and weep for us, because of the fact that we are so fleshly and worldly; self-centred, self-serving and self-seeking. We are nothing but slaves to our emotions and to carnality.

You cannot believe how many people, so-called believers, in America, believe we are more spiritual and more mature than most other people in other countries! This could not be further from the truth. God has allowed me to be in the midst of other believers in poverty-stricken countries, where they have nothing, yet many of them are more spiritually mature then we are. They literally put us to shame! **May God have mercy on our souls.**

#24 AGAINST ALL ODDS – A 30 FOOT UPLINK SATELLITE SYSTEM

When God told me to buy a **C-band uplink system** (originally $250,000) that my friend had faxed to me. I contacted the broker and made arrangements to purchase the uplink system. As the money came in through the following weeks, we wired the money into a Westinghouse account. During this time, we also applied for our C-band uplink license through the FCC. Westinghouse sent us the blueprints we needed to begin to prepare and pour the foundation. I think there was over fifteen yards of concrete alone that we needed to pour. That was not including the precise placement of hundreds of rebars, which needed to be placed into the concrete pad - before we could pick up the dish.

Westinghouse informed me that where the satellite uplink system was located was a very wet area, and if there was any type of water on the ground when we tried to take a crane or an 18 wheel truck back into that area, it would sink - up to its windshield. They insisted it must be a very dry time before I could pick it up. I shared this with the whole congregation, so that we could believe for the dry spell that we desperately needed. As we came into the fall, rain began to fall heavily all the way from out West to the East Coast. It rained, and rained, and rained!! On the Saturday, right before Thanksgiving, the **Spirit of the Lord spoke to me** - out of nowhere - and told me it was time to go get the uplink system. **I knew it was the voice of God,** so I contacted the men in my church who had volunteered to help pick up the equipment. (What I'm about to share with you could be a book in and by itself, so I will try to keep it brief.)

The men I had contacted to help me go pick up the system, challenged me a little about going. Nevertheless, they had been with me through numerous life storms, and they knew that I could hear from God. I told them to come to the Sunday morning church service and be prepared to leave right after the service. We had a Dodge Caravan, that six of us could cram into, with an attached covered trailer that would carry our air compressor and tools. That Sunday morning I informed the congregation of our intentions to go pick up the satellite uplink system. Some of the people became extremely upset - since it had been raining for weeks on end. After all, I had verbally told them that we could not pick up the system unless we had a thoroughly **dry season**. On top of that, we were still $8,000 short of the money we needed to complete the transaction! However, I told the congregation that I knew in my heart that the Lord had spoken to me, so we would be going.

We are talking close to a 1,400 mile trip. If I had not heard from heaven correctly … we were in big trouble! As we pulled out of the parking lot that Sunday afternoon, it was cold, wet, and raining everywhere. All through the day we drove in the rain. We did not stop through the night, but drove straight through to the next day. As we pulled into State College, Texas, it was still raining. I told the men, even though it's the end of the day, let's go look at the **C-band uplink system**. We followed the directions to the Westinghouse factory. As we pulled onto the property, something really strange seemed wrong with their yard. All of their grass was **brown and dead**. We pulled up to a parking spot right outside of the main office; then we went inside to introduce ourselves to the personnel.

There was a woman behind a glass sliding window at a countertop. We commented to her about the grass being brown and dead on their property. She told us it was the strangest thing that they had ever seen or experienced. It had rained everywhere else in their area, but not one drop of rain had fallen upon the Westinghouse ground. There was absolutely no explanation for it. At least that's what they believed, we knew different! We were smack-dab, right in the middle of the will of God and God had kept their land dry.

#25 Miracles According to His Will

The Westinghouse factory informed us that the C-band uplink system was around the back. However, it was going to take special equipment to dismantle this sophisticated piece of equipment. One company had told them it would take about a week to dismantle, with the cost of $40,000. Well ... we were all just a bunch of country hicks with an air compressor and regular tools! They also informed us we would need a large crane, with a specially-designed truck, to carry the equipment. In addition, it would be impossible during this particular week, because it was Thanksgiving. They also informed us that they would need to have all the money wired into their account – in advance - before we would even be allowed to touch, let alone disassemble, the system.

I told them this was acceptable to us, because we needed a good night's sleep anyway, and we would be back early in the morning to dismantle the system: in order to have it shipped to our facility in Gettysburg, Pennsylvania. Some of the men asked me what we were going to do, because we did not have the money, the equipment, nor did we have the truck. I told them everything was okay.

The gift of FAITH was at work in my heart

I called up the church office, just to double check about the $8,000 that we still needed, and they informed me nothing had come in, as of yet.

Even though I had been informed that the $8,000 we needed still had not come in, we were up bright and early. We headed out to have a good breakfast before arriving at Westinghouse. I called up our church office, after 8:00 a.m. EST, to ask if the money was there yet. They said: **"No Pastor, there is no sign of it ... and we don't know what to tell you."** I told them that it was okay. That we did not need the money until we got to the factory to pick up the equipment.

We arrived at the factory, walked up to the front office counter, and informed them that we were ready to begin dismantling the uplink satellite system. They said that there was still a problem - with us being short $8,000. I told them to access their account and they would discover the money had been wired. The lady went to her computer and came back a few minutes later and said, **"Yes, it had just been wired." Hallelujah!** The money had been wired to Westinghouse's account! To this day, I am not certain where all the money came from, but God had supplied.

We drove the minivan and trailer to the uplink system. It was one *big* satellite dish. (You can come and see it at our church.) I had all the men gathered together in a circle, holding hands to pray. I prayed that God would give to us a spirit of wisdom and understanding in the knowledge of what we needed to do, and how to do it, quickly and speedily - with no damage to the system! After we were done praying and thanking God, I discussed with the men what needed to happen next.

The Spirit of God came upon all of us. I began to watch the men crawl over the satellite dish; like a well-organized and experienced team. It was so amazing, that the personnel, technicians, and scientists came out of the Westinghouse factory to watch us. They were snapping pictures as we were working! They were absolutely flabbergasted and kept talking about how it was supposed to take a week for the dish to be disassembled and packed - not two days!

As our men were working, I began to make phone calls. The Lord provided a crane company to come for the day. Of course, once they arrived they tried to charge us way more than what they agreed upon over the phone. But God gave me gentle, holy boldness to deal with it. So, they eventually came back down to their original verbal agreement. I then contacted a trucking terminal out of Houston, Texas and told them the kind of truck we were looking for. They informed me that they did not have that type of truck available; and they did not know where to send us to find one. Not only that, but there was nobody there, being only a couple of days before Thanksgiving. I asked them to please just go ahead and look around.

The man on the phone said: "Hold on! There's a man and woman standing outside of my office right now. I need to ask them what they want." To his amazement, they were a married couple looking to carry a load back East. He put the man on the phone with me. Amazingly, it was exactly the kind of truck we desperately needed! The couple arrived with the truck and backed up to the large satellite dish. The truck did not sink down in the least, because the ground was so dry, and hard.

The panels of the uplink dish were all stacked off to the side, so we only needed the crane for one day. All the crane had to do was load up the main pedestal and the transmission shed.

The next morning we came back to finish the packing. We had a wonderful time sharing Christ with the married couple that owned the truck. I am convinced that both of them are probably saved now, because we asked if we could pray for them before they left with our equipment. I saw the gift of faith come upon them as we laid our hands on them.

We loaded the truck and found that the transmitter building itself was too tall to fit under the bridges. Not only was the equipment too high to fit under bridges, and overpasses, but our satellite equipment succeeded the legal weight limit of what the truck was allowed to carry. We told the couple that we did not know what we could do, but that we'd certainly be praying for them. The driver informed us not to worry about them getting our equipment to us.

How he brought our uplink system to Pennsylvania is another amazing story in itself. As he was driving his truck on the main highways, he would slow down as he approached a bridge, and let the air out of his air shocks. He'd crawl slowly under the bridge and would speak to other truck drivers by CB, those who were ahead of him, to find out if the weigh stations were open. If they were open, he would pull over until they had too many 18 wheelers to inspect, and then he'd pass by safely. He did this all the way from Texas to Gettysburg, Pennsylvania!

When the uplink dish finally arrived, we had a crew of men and women ready. The huge concrete slab, which was over three feet deep, and the rebar that was needed in the concrete was cured and ready. Within three days we had this system installed, ready to operate, and ready to broadcast. However, the time to broadcast was not immediate.

> *Romans 8:27-28 And he that searcheth the hearts knoweth what is the mind of the Spirit, because he maketh intercession for the saints according to the will of God. 28 And we know that all things work together for good to them that love God, to them who are the called according to his purpose.*

#26 How We Became The Largest Christian Broadcasters On The Internet! (1996)

In 1983, the Lord had us begin "Jesus is Lord Ministries International." That same year, I heard the audible voice of God telling me to go on TV. He gave me the exact station, time, day, and hour that I would be broadcasting. All that the Lord had spoken to me came to pass. From then, to now, we have been actively involved in broadcast media for the propagation of the gospel around the world. God has allowed us to own numerous radio stations throughout the years. We have also broadcast by satellite, with our own C-Band Uplink system. We have broadcast on many TV stations, including low power TV stations, our own

KA band satellite TV network. At one time, we were broadcasting five days a week, with Dr. Lester Sumrall's satellite network: LeSEA Broadcasting Network!

In the mid-1990s, I was contemplating purchasing channel 68, which is a local TV station, when the Lord spoke to my heart and told me not to buy any TV stations: because the Internet was going to become the number one vessel to reach the world.

I moved in the divine revelation God had given to me. The church I pastor, and oversee, **Jesus is Lord Ministries International,** made a sizable investment into the broadcasting of the gospel, by the Internet; beginning with a T-1 line. In that season, there was only one other ministry we were aware of, that was doing live-streaming, archiving, and making time available for other ministers. God quickened my heart to provide a platform by which ministers, who were preaching the truth, could reach the world by Internet. Immediately, God began to give us favor with some of the best-known ministers. Some of these ministers were: **Joyce Meyer, Charles Capps, Kenneth Hagin, Sid Roth etc**.

For a season, God allowed us to become the largest broadcaster in new technology, that carried live-streaming & archiving of programs.

In 1975, the Lord spoke to my heart and revealed that I would be involved in providing a platform in which ministers could speak to the nations. Our broadcasts reach people all around the world, by all the latest and modern technology. You can still watch us by going to: www.WBNTV.ORG

#27 God Spoke To My Heart To Broadcast Across USA! (2002)

$250,000 contract. No income. No ministers. Inoperable equipment.

The church sanctuary could sit over seven-hundred people; but our congregation had dropped to approximately thirty. The Lord was teaching me how to trust Him. One day, as I was in prayer in our sanctuary, the Holy Spirit spoke to my heart: "Begin to broadcast by satellite twenty-four hours a day." It was about five years after we had installed our C-band uplink system and we had a license with the FCC for this 9 Meter Earth satellite system. I had tried and tried to bring us online, but never succeeded. Now, when we had just a little congregation, no ministers, no finances, no technicians--- the Lord spoke to me, and said: "Do it now!" I knew, that I knew, that I knew, this was from God. I called up NPR, out of Washington DC, and told them I wanted to buy satellite time.

I also contacted a company by the name of ANTEC, out of Frederick, Maryland. I made arrangements to meet with both of these companies: NPR would provide the satellite time and ANTEC would help us bring our uplink system online. Two men from NPR met me in my office and put a contract in front of me. It was a $250,000, two-year contract! It was going to cost us $12,000 per month to broadcast on their satellite transponder. The Spirit of the Lord quickened my heart and said: "Sign it!" We had no ministers to broadcast with us and no natural source of income. NPR was only giving us one month to do test patterns, and to begin to broadcast. I signed the $250,000 contract by faith.

#28 Shooting Into The Dark 22,000 Miles Up!

The technicians from ANTEC (Frederick, MD) came to our facilities. They looked over our system and informed us that it was a good system. They asked who had installed the system for us and we told them how it all happened. Not only did we take down the extremely expensive and complicated system, but we also reassembled it with non-technical volunteers. They looked at us with unbelief! They said the tuning of the dish was a highly technical endeavour, and even if it needed just a little bit of work, we'd be talking approximately $10,000.

I asked the gentleman in charge, John, if they would bring it online and try to broadcast with it - the way it was. He said he could, but there was no doubt it probably needed some major work. We installed all of the necessary equipment and he set-up his test equipment. It was 22,000 miles to the satellite we'd be broadcasting from, and the dish must be perfectly tuned. I left them to do their work and went back to my office.

After a couple of hours, John called and asked me to go to the transmission building. When I walked into the building, the technicians were crouching over the spectroscopes, waveform monitors, meters and equipment. John looked up at me with total surprise and astonishment on his face. He asked me to come over and take a look at one of the spectroscopes. I saw perfect waves moving across the screen. He said, to their complete surprise, the vertex satellite dish was perfectly aligned and tuned, and we did not have to pay for an expensive retooling and re-tuning. This was completely unheard of in their industry!

Within one month, God supernaturally sent us quality ministers. We began to broadcast twenty-four hours a day. We renegotiated our contract, about halfway through, and they gave us a better price. After three years of broadcasting by satellite, which went to low power TV stations, TV stations and the Sky Angel network; we came off the air. ANTEC approached us - to purchase our equipment. But, I believe, with all my heart, that God is not yet done with the Word Broadcasting Network.

#29 We Gave Away 80,000 Cassettes And CDs (2001)

My wife sometimes gets upset with me, because I give everything away. The first book I had printed (1996) was: **"War in the Heavenlies."** I had 10,000 copies printed and I probably gave away two-thirds of them. I just can't help it! I want people to experience the fullness of Christ. I want them to be free, to grow spiritually, and so I give away that which I believe will help them grow spiritually.

Back in 2001, we were doing evangelistic outreaches throughout Pennsylvania, Maryland, and Delaware. It was in my heart to leave something in their hands. The income from the church was almost non-existent, and yet, somehow, God kept us going. I put my faith out there to purchase CD duplicators plus cassette duplicators. My three sons and I began to mass-produce CDs and cassettes. Most of the messages were not from me, but other ministers, who I believed had powerful messages that would transform people's lives. The teachings were not copyrighted materials - so all we did was legal. Wherever we went, we began to pass out CDs and cassettes.

It was in my heart to reach even more people; so we went to many different stores, getting permission to put clear plastic bowls on their counters. On these bowls was a very nice label that declared: "Free Teaching Cassette!" We would try to revisit those stores, once or twice a month, to restock them with more teachings. We estimate that within a two-year period, over **80,000 cassettes and CDs** were passed out.

You might ask: "Did it increase the attendance of your church?" No. But that was never the object. We simply wanted to see people set free, and follow Jesus Christ. Where did we get all the money for the CDs and cassettes? I'll be honest with you, I do not know. It had to be God! We simply began to step out in obedience, trying to fulfil the great commission. Yes, we were preaching on the streets, singing, and passing out tracts, but that wasn't enough. We needed to leave something in people's hands; something they could listen to. We will never know, on this side of heaven, if what we did had any effect. When we get to glory we will discover the results. Remember, God's Word never returns void!

Isaiah 55:11 So shall my word be that goeth forth out of my mouth: it shall not return unto me void, but it shall accomplish that which I please, and it shall prosper in the thing whereto I sent it.

#30 Raising The Dead At Cracker Barrel! (2016)

In mid-November, 2016, my wife asked me to take her for breakfast at Cracker Barrel. I agreed to her request, and informed her that I would love to go and eat breakfast with her at Cracker Barrel. From where I pastor, in Gettysburg, PA, it is roughly a twenty-minute drive. We arrived at Cracker Barrel around 10 a.m. One of the waitresses took us to our table, which was in the middle of the restaurant; and we were sat, simply discussing how good and wonderful God has been to us before we ordered our breakfast.

Eventually, the food arrived and my wife and I held hands and thanked God for our food and His divine guidance in our lives. Two waitresses suddenly appeared, and urgently walked down the length of the restaurant; asking if there were any doctors or nurses available. We could tell that something urgent and tragic was happening by the way they were calling out for help.

In most of these similar situations I would be immediately on my feet heading to the problem area. One time, I was at Lowe's, with my family, shopping, when a similar situation happened. One of the tellers had gone into an epileptic seizure. I immediately ran over to the counter and informed them that I was a doctor (Ph.D. in Biblical Theology) and that I could help. In that situation, I simply leaned over the counter, and laid my hand on the girl having the seizure. She was thrashing about and I took authority, very quietly, commanding the devil to loose her and let her go. Immediately, the seizure stopped - and she jumped up to her feet.

Now, here I was, in a seemingly similar situation. What is so strange though, is that I did not sense any urgency in my heart to go and help at that moment. It did not occur to me - until after the event - that for some reason, I had not acted in my regular and routine method. Now that I look back, I believe God was in this. My wife and I simply sat there, talking back and forth a little bit, and finished our meal.

Approximately ten minutes later, we simply got to our feet and walked towards the front of the restaurant. As we got closer to the entrance of the restaurant, we that noticed a small crowd had gathered. We walked up to the crowd and I could see that there was a woman leaning over the top of another woman; a rather large lady. The lady was lying on her left side, on the floor, and her body was completely extended out. She seemed to be completely still. There was no movement from her whatsoever. And there was a heavy blanket of silence over the whole crowd.

When I saw the lady lying on the floor, the compassion of God rose up in my heart, and I was motivated to get involved. I walked over to the crowd and very gently pushed my way through, I spoke up and informed the crowd that I was a local pastor and I would like to help.

The woman, who was bending over the lady lying on the floor, informed me that she was a nurse. She had a hold of one of the hands of the lady lying on the floor. I could see that the nurse had her fingers on that lady's wrist: looking for a heartbeat. I knelt down next to her. The lady, on the floor, looked to be in her mid-60s. She was completely still. Tears began to fill my eyes, and I reached forth my hand and placed it upon her cheek. I discovered that her cheek was extremely cold.

I have learned in these situations we do not have to pray a loud prayer, or shout at the enemy. With the love of God flowing in my heart, I prayed a very simple prayer in Jesus name. I commanded the spirit of infirmity to go, and began speaking life over her, very quietly, in Jesus name. As I prayed for this lady, tears were once again filling my eyes. I felt as if I knew her personally, and that she was someone who was important to me. This is how the Holy Spirit works, God has shed His love abroad in our hearts by the Holy Ghost.

As I continued praying, the nurse became excited and said: "She has a Pulse!" (When I thought about it later, it became obvious to me: up to that moment this lady had lost her pulse!) I continued to pray softly ... the lady began to stir. I still had my right hand laid very softly on her cheek. The next thing I knew, this lady reached up her right hand and put it on my hand.

I knew, in my heart, that my job was done. The Spirit of Christ had touched this precious lady and raised her from the dead! There were no fireworks, explosions, or loud shouting; but simply the gentle moving of the spirit of Christ. The Resurrection Power of God manifested - without people even realizing it.

I got up from my kneeling position and walked back to the crowd, where my wife waited for me to simply complete the task. As we walked out the door of Cracker Barrel, the ambulance was coming around the corner - with its lights flashing. We simply got into our car and drove away, knowing that once again, God had confirmed the authority that we have in the Name of Jesus, with signs following.

#31 Arthritis Could Not Stay (1996-present)

There are generational curses that are passed on from one generation to the next. These are satanic strongholds that must be broken! In my family lineage, there were quite a number of these strongholds. My family members, and myself, have had numerous physical infirmities.

When I gave my heart to Jesus Christ, and began to intensely study the Word of God, I discovered that I was free from the curse of the law. I began to aggressively take what Christ had purchased for me with the stripes on His back. By faith, I began to cast down the physical strongholds. Not only did I receive healing for my own body, but I also declared in the name of Jesus, these physical afflictions would not be passed on any longer. My sons and daughters, and their children would not have these afflictions.

One of the afflictions that has been passed on, from generation to generation, is arthritis. My sister, Deborah, began to experience arthritis in her late 20s. She was a very gifted typist and piano player. However, before she was in her 40s her fingers had become gnarled and almost unusable. Arthritis had entered her body so dramatically that I remember her crying with pain and great suffering.

By my late 20s, and early 30s, arthritis began to try and manifest itself in the joints of my fingers too. The minute that pain came into my hands, I began to boldly speak to them; even as Jesus declared in the Gospel of Mark 11:23:

Mark 11:23 For verily I say unto you, That whosoever shall say unto this mountain, Be thou removed, and be thou cast into the sea; and shall not doubt in his heart, but shall believe that those things which he saith shall come to pass; he shall have whatsoever he saith.

I submitted myself to God and I resisted the devil, by speaking to the affliction and commanding it to go. Then, I praised God and thanked Him that by faith I was healed In the Name of Jesus: no matter how my hands or fingers felt! I thank God that I was healed.

Sure enough, after a day or two, the stiffening and pain completely dissipated from my joints. Through the years, it has tried to come back - over and over - but I have not allowed it to! I know this may sound braggadocios, but it's not. This is a reality that Christ has given to every believer

#32 HOW I Received Healing For A Broken Kneecap!
(1988)

We had a very heavy snowfall in the winter of 1988. I

owned an old John Deere snowmobile, that I made available to the local fire department; if they ever needed my help. Eventually, they called me up, during one terrible winter storm, and told me they had a heavy equipment operator that needed to be transported to Orrtanna, PA.

He needed to be picked up at his house and transported for about six miles. I informed the fire department that I would be more than willing to do this for them, especially because I love adventures! Actually, I'm a snow addict! I can never get enough snow. The snowstorm and sleet had not yet abated and was raging in all its fury. So, I told my wife, Kathleen, that the fire department had just called and had a job for me to do ... Mike to the rescue! Or so I thought. I dressed up in all my winter trappings, went outside, brushed the snow off my snowmobile, and laid my hands on it: commanding it not to give me any problems! I should have prayed over myself first. I started the old machine up, and revved the throttle as I headed out of the church parking lot. I turned to my right and went down the deserted, main highway. There I was, having the time of my life - and doing it for the fire department! I was going about fifty miles an hour (or faster) when I hit a section that was nothing but black ice!

The back end of the snowmobile spun to the right - out of control! I went flying through the air as it threw me for a lopper. I slammed my right kneecap extremely hard on the asphalt road. I felt my kneecap rip, break, and tear as I went sliding down the road ... for quite a distance. Meanwhile, the snowmobile continued on its way, spinning out of control. It eventually stopped, because my hand was no longer cranking the throttle. Fortunately, it was not damaged, because there was nothing but snow in every direction. There I was, lying on the road, in the snow, and freezing wind, clutching my busted up knee. I was alone and in tremendous pain! Immediately, I cried out to Jesus and repented for being so stupid - and for not using Godly wisdom.

My theology is: Almost everything that goes wrong in my life is usually my own stupid fault. Even if the devil is involved, it is most likely, because I first opened the door for him. After I was done repenting and confessing to the Lord; I went aggressively after my healing. I commanded my kneecap to be put back into its normal condition in the name of Jesus Christ of Nazareth. I commanded every broken part of it to be made whole. You see, I could grab my patella, and move it all around. It was no longer attached to my knee! It seemed to have become completely disconnected - no longer restrained by its associated ligaments.

Probably, at this juncture most people would have called it quits, when it comes to completing the mission they set out on. But, that is not my mode of operation. If I declared that I was healed - then I needed to act upon it! I discovered a truth a long time ago: God cannot lie! So, I slowly crawled back over to my snowmobile, and pulled myself back into the seat. I painfully swung my right leg over the seat, into its proper position. At that moment, wave after wave of pain overwhelmed me. Years of experience of walking in faith, however, caused me to declare that I was healed in the name of Jesus: "In the name of Jesus, I am healed!" I opened the throttle and proceeded to pick up the equipment operator. All the time, I continually proclaimed the truth.

On the way, there were many areas that my snowmobile just would not go: the snow was way too deep or the roads were flooded with water. The storm had dumped a combination of rain, ice, and snow. I would need a boat to go through some of these areas! Admittedly, at times, I took chances that I should not have taken. I would accelerate to a high speed and just zip across the flooded areas. The back end of the snowmobile would begin to sink, as if I wasn't going to make it. But, I would constantly revert back to my old trusted declaration: "In the name of Jesus, in the name of Jesus, in the name of Jesus, I will make it!" There are a lot of wonderful messages preached on faith - but that's not what wins the victory. It is when the Word has been quickened in your heart that you know, that you know, that you know, that you know that God and His

Word are true.

I cannot describe enough the immense pain and agony that I was experiencing, yet I did not merely think I was healed: I knew I was healed! Faith is not thinking, hoping, or wishing. It is knowing! You know, that you know, that you know!

So, I finally reached my first destination. The township worker saw me pull up outside of his house. As he approached the snowmobile, he could not see my face: because of my helmet and ski mask. I did not tell him that I'd had an accident ... and possibly shattered my kneecap. I do not adhere to bragging about the devil or his shenanigans, lies or deceptions. This was no little man that I had to carry on the back of my snowmobile either. He mounted up and we were on our way. It took major faith to keep on going. We had to take numerous detours before I finally got him to the big earthmover machine that he was tasked to operate. He jumped off my snowmobile and thanked me for the ride. I told him it was no problem as I opened up the throttle and headed off home.

This time, I decided to take a different route, because the last route was so bad. It took all the faith that I could muster to get back to the parsonage. I was cold, wet, tired and completely overwhelmed with pain. When I got home I just kept on thanking God that I was healed. During the next couple of days, I refused to pamper my leg. I did not put any ice or heat upon it. I did not take any kind of medication or painkillers. I did not call anyone asking them to please pray for me and believe God for my healing. I know this may seem extremely stupid, but I knew, in my heart, that I was healed. It has got to be in your heart! My head, my body, and my throbbing and busted kneecap were all telling me that I was not healed, but let God's Word be true and every symptom a lie! When the next Sunday rolled around the roads were clear enough for people to make it to church.

During that time, you might have called me Hop-along Cassidy, because of the way I was walking. I did not deny the problem, but I sure as heaven denied the right for it to exist! One of our parishioners, a nurse, saw me limping badly. She asked me what happened and I told her. She informed me that this was a major problem, and tried to explain (in medical terms) exactly what she thought I had done to my knee. Medically, in order to reattach and repair my patella, I would have to endure at least one major surgical procedure. She recounted to me that she once had a similar injury, although it was nowhere near as bad as mine. She went on to elaborate that even after an extensive operation, her knee was still giving her major problems. I thanked her for this information, and went back to trusting and believing that by the stripes of Jesus Christ, I was healed.

I sure as heaven was not going to let go - or give up - on God's Promises! I wrestled with this situation day after day: commanding my knee to be healed and to function as God had designed it to. When the pain overwhelmed me, I would tell it to shut up, be quiet and work! When it seemed like my leg would not carry me, I would command it to be strong in the name of Jesus. This went on for over a month. One morning, I crawled out of bed, and my kneecap was perfectly healed! You would think that when the healing manifested I would begin to sing, shout and dance; but I did not, and I do not! You see, I had already done all of my rejoicing, in advance, because I believed that the minute I prayed, I received!

CHAPTER SEVEN

Strong FAITH Comes By The Sacrifice Of Praise & Thanksgiving

Many ministers today are declaring that everything that happens to people is God's fault. This is one of the most grievous and ridiculous lies propagated by the devil. People teach that God is in control of everything, which, is absolutely not the truth. Yes, if God so desired, He could stop humanity in its tracks: and He will someday. But, at this moment in time, He has given us a choice to make: we can choose to follow Him, or disobey. And based upon these decisions we will reap either life or death! When people declare that God is in control of everything, it simply reveals their utter ignorance of the workings and dealings of God.

Many bad things take place because we do not submit to, yield to, or stay in obedience to the Lord. It is also because many people are ignorant of God's will; or they are not taking the authority which is given to us. *John 10:10: "The thief cometh not, but for to steal, and to kill, and to destroy:"* But, Jesus said: *"I am come that they might have life, and that they might have it more abundantly."* We overcome the world, the flesh and the devil by faith in **Jesus Christ**!

The purpose of this book is to help you to walk in the audacious Faith that is in **Christ Jesus**! Many people have realized that they need an education to be successful in this world; so they pay whatever price they need to, and do whatever it takes to get an education. Many people today are in desperate need of medical help, and they are willing to do whatever it takes to get better. There are many other examples I could use, pertaining to people giving all that they have, in order to possess something they need. However, the greatest need of all is for us to have faith in **Christ**.

1 John 5:3-5 For this is the love of God, that we keep his commandments: and his commandments are not grievous. 4 For whatsoever is born of God overcometh the world: and this is the victory that overcometh the world, even our faith. 5 Who is he that overcometh the world, but he that believeth that Jesus is the Son of God?

God has given to us amazing tools, weapons, and spiritual truths: in order that we might become partakers of His divine nature. His divine nature will only be manifested in us to the degree of our Faith in **Christ Jesus**.

Hebrews 13:15 By him therefore let us offer the <u>sacrifice</u> of praise to God continually, that is, the fruit of our lips giving thanks to his name.

Notice the word 'sacrifice' in this Scripture. Hebrews is a tremendous book that reveals the sacrifice **Christ** made for our salvation. The Book of Hebrews also reveals that God requires us to continue to make sacrifices, not as in the old covenant (with the shedding of the blood of animals) but in our lives and by our conduct. It takes faith to **give thanks and praise to God** when the natural world tells us there seems to be no reason why we should rejoice. I can honestly tell you, this has been one of the number one ways God has allowed me to receive many miracles.

As I have rejoiced, praised, thanked and worshipped God in the midst of hardship: faith has risen up within my heart in order for me to possess that which God has promised. At the end of this chapter, I will share with you numerous experiences that I've had, over a forty year period, pertaining to this truth.

In the old covenant, sacrifices were extremely important: beginning with Able, Abraham, Isaac, Jacob, and all the patriarchs of old. The sacrifice of praise and thanksgiving is extremely important in the development of our faith in **Christ Jesus**. Let us take a moment to look at some of the definitions for the words revealed to us in verse 15.

Praise: To speak highly of, complement, applaud, give a standing ovation to, salute; or we could simply say: "YEA" to Jesus!

A sacrifice will always cost something that our flesh will not want to give. My emotions and feelings do not want to praise God in the midst of dire circumstances and terrible situations. But if I simply do this, by faith, it brings about a miraculous change in me: which brings Glory to the **Father**. This will be well pleasing to our Heavenly **Father** and causes God to take notice of us. You see, faith has a divine fragrance that attracts the attention of heaven. This is not, in any way exaggerated but absolute truth. God is looking for those people whose hearts are in agreement (in faith) with Him!

2 Chronicles 16:9 For the eyes of the Lord run to and fro throughout the whole earth, to shew himself strong in the behalf of them whose heart is perfect toward him ...

Hebrews 13:15 also tells us we are to offer unto God the sacrifice continually! It is not to be spasmodic, temporary, or only when we feel like it; but continually offer unto God praise and thanksgiving. Let's take a closer look at the word "continually."

Continually: At all times, endlessly, always, occurring without stopping, evermore, forevermore, perpetually, on a regular basis.

The use of the word "**continually**" implies that it must be a daily, moment by moment, lifestyle. I cannot emphasize the importance of this act of faith sufficiently. Many people are defeated - simply because they will not obey the Word of God! Faith cannot, and will not, grow in an atmosphere of disobedience.

Psalm 34:1 I will bless the Lord at all times: his praise shall continually be in my mouth.

Acts 16:25 And at midnight Paul and Silas prayed, and sang praises unto God: and the prisoners heard them.

Ephesians 5:20 Giving thanks always for all things unto God and the Father in the name of our Lord Jesus Christ;

Psalm 145:1-2 I will extol thee, my God, O king; and I will bless thy name for ever and ever. 2 Every day will I bless thee; and I will praise thy name for ever and ever.

1 Thessalonians 5:18 In every thing give thanks: for this is the will of God in Christ Jesus concerning you.

Colossians 3:17 And whatsoever ye do in word or deed, do all in the name of the Lord Jesus, giving thanks to God and the Father by him.

Psalm 71:8 Let my mouth be filled with thy praise and with thy honour all the day.

Let us take a look at another set of very important Scriptures:

Colossians 2:5-7 For though I be absent in the flesh, yet am I with you in the spirit, joying and beholding your order, and the stedfastness of your faith in Christ. 6 As ye have therefore received Christ Jesus the Lord, so walk ye in him: 7 Rooted and built up in him, and stablished in the faith, as ye have been taught, abounding therein with thanksgiving.

Our roots must go deep into **Christ**. He is the vine, and we are the branches. All of our life flows from **Christ** into us, into every fiber of our being. **Christ** lives in our hearts, by faith, this is why it is so important that our faith in **Jesus Christ** must increase on a daily, and a moment by moment, basis. Please notice that Paul the Apostle said "abounding therein with **Thanksgiving.**" This is an amazing revelation! If you will take a hold of this truth, it will transform your life! The definition of abounding:

overflowing, increasing, multiplication. There are many Scriptures that confirm this in the New Testament and in the Old Testament.

Psalm 23:5 Thou preparest a table before me in the presence of mine enemies: thou anointest my head with oil; my cup runneth over.

How was David's cup running over? He was constantly giving thanks to God. The Scriptures declare that the people who consistently, moment by moment, give thanks unto God - no matter the circumstances - are constantly partaking of a continual feast.

Proverbs 15:15 All the days of the afflicted are evil: but he that is of a merry heart hath a continual feast.

Thanksgiving reveals a heart that is filled with appreciation, gratitude and gratefulness. This is actually an expression of faith.

'Lord, I Thank You' sang by Andraè Crouch is one of my favorite songs. Not only is it faith in action, but it will cause you to literally take off like a rocket in the development of your faith.

Acts 16:23-26 And when they had laid many stripes upon them, they cast them into prison, charging the jailor to keep them safely: 24 Who, having received such a charge, thrust them into the inner prison, and made their feet fast in the stocks. 25 And at midnight Paul and Silas prayed, and sang praises unto God: and the prisoners heard them. 26 And suddenly there was a great earthquake, so that the foundations of the prison were shaken: and immediately all the doors were opened, and every one's bands were loosed.

Not only did Paul and Silas operate in the realm of **Faith**, but through this experience their **Faith** had a sudden spurt of growth. When we operate in faith, God will always, supernaturally, and divinely, intervene and show up. Let us look at another Scripture.

Psalm 100:4 Enter into his gates with thanksgiving, and into his courts with praise: be thankful unto him, and bless his name.

We can expand on this Scripture a little bit, even change it slightly, to have a correct understanding and interpretation. Let's do that for a moment:

Psalm 100:4 Enter into his gates (of faith) with thanksgiving, and into his courts (of trust) with praise: be thankful unto him, and bless his name.

With the sacrifice of praise and thanksgiving, we enter into a new world: the divine, spiritual world of the heavenly realm - where all things are possible!

Psalm 100:3-5 Know ye that the LORD he is God: it is he that hath made us, and not we ourselves; we are his people, and the sheep of his pasture. 4 Enter into his gates with thanksgiving, and into his courts with praise: be thankful unto him, and bless his name. 5 For the Lord is good; his mercy is everlasting; and his truth endureth to all generations.

This is why our hearts should be filled with thanksgiving and praise: the **Lord** is good! Yes, good! And His mercy is everlasting. Let the sacrifice of thanksgiving flow out of our belly, like rivers of living water. Then there will rise up within us a faith that will overcome the world, the flesh, and the devil. Our faith cannot help but grow when our hearts are filled with the atmosphere of praise, and thanksgiving.

The flip side of the coin is: unbelief cannot help but grow, like a weed, when there is grumbling, griping, complaining, faultfinding, unappreciative and thankless hearts. With over forty years of ministry behind me, I cannot believe how many people I run into that call themselves Christians who are grumblers, gripers, complainers, faultfinders and just simply negative people. And yet they do not understand why they are living such defeated lives?!

Colossians 1:12 <u>Giving thanks </u> unto the Father, which hath made us meet to be partakers of the inheritance of the saints in light:

Colossians 3:15-17 And let the peace of God rule in your hearts, to the which also ye are called in one body; and be ye <u>thankful</u>. 16 Let the word of Christ dwell in you richly in all wisdom; teaching and admonishing one another in psalms and hymns and spiritual songs, singing with grace in your hearts to the Lord. 17 And whatsoever ye do in word or deed, do all in the name of the Lord Jesus, <u>giving thanks</u> to God and the Father by him.

The Word of God is full of Scriptures commanding us to give thanks: over and over! This is good, rich, soil in which your faith will grow exceedingly, and become strong and great in **Christ Jesus**.

1 Thessalonians 5:18 In every thing give thanks: for this is the will of God in Christ Jesus concerning you.

Ephesians 5:20 Giving thanks always for all things unto God and the Father in the name of our Lord Jesus Christ;

Philippians 4:6 Be careful for nothing; but in every thing by prayer and supplication with thanksgiving let your requests be made known unto God.

Psalm 34:1 I will bless the Lord at all times: his praise shall continually be in my mouth.

Psalm 95:2 Let us come before his presence with thanksgiving, and make a joyful noise unto him with psalms.

Psalm 100:2 Serve the LORD with gladness: come before his presence with singing.

Believe me, there are hundreds of stories I could share with you here. This is only one of them!

#33 Victory Over Tumors By Sacrifice Of Thanksgiving!

I woke up one morning with tremendous pain in my lower abdomen. As I lifted up my shirt, and looked down to where the pain was, I noticed there was a lump on my abdomen - about the size of an acorn. I laid my hands on it immediately and commanded it to go.

I said: "You lying devil! By the stripes of **Jesus** I am healed and made whole." After I'd spoken to the lump, the pain became excruciating, overwhelmingly worse. That whole day, I walked the floor, crying out to God. I praised Him and thanked Him that His Word is real and true. I went for a walk, on the mountain right behind the parsonage. It was a long day - before I got to sleep that night. When I awoke the next morning, the pain was even more severe! It felt like somebody was stabbing me in my gut with a knife. I lifted up my shirt and looked ... there was another lump.

So, now I had two lumps in my lower abdomen! I laid my hands on them and commanded them to go. Tears were rolling down my face, as I spoke the Word. I lifted my hands toward heaven and kept praising God that I was healed. Even though I did not see any change, I kept on praising God! All the symptoms were telling me that God's Word is a lie, and that I was not healed by the stripes of **Jesus**. But I knew that I was healed! It was another long day, and it seemed as if I would never get to sleep that night. The pain was continual and non-stop.

When I got up the next morning the pain had intensified - even more! Once again, I looked at my abdomen ... and to my shock there was yet another lump! Now I had three of these nasty lumps! Each one was about the size of an acorn. I did not think that the pain could get any worse - but it did. Yet again, I laid my hands on these tumors and commanded them to go in the name of **Jesus**

Christ of Nazareth.

I declared that by the stripes of **Jesus** I am healed! All that day and night, it felt like there was a knife sticking in my gut. I lifted my hands, and with tears rolling down my face (again!) I kept on praising God that I was healed! By faith, I began to dance before the Lord. It was a victory dance! I continually praised God that I was healed by the stripes of **Jesus**. I went to bed that night hurting worse than ever. All night long I tossed and turned, moaned and groaned; yet all the time I persisted in thanking God that I was not going to die, but that I was healed! I got up the next morning and all of the pain had gone. I checked my abdomen …all of the tumors were gone! Furthermore, they have never come back!!

#34 Thanking God For Food & Money We Did Not Have!

I got up early in the morning - as per my usual routine - it was time for me to talk to God: about our needs. We were in Germany at this time, doing missionary work. We were also completely out of food, money and gas for our car. Our one-year-old son was having to depend on mom for all of his nourishment. The apartment we were staying in, at this time, had a long hallway leading to all rooms: straight ahead was a very small front room (with sliding doors); on the right-hand was a small kitchen and on the left-hand was the bedroom.

I was in the front room praying and crying out to God. I never complain, gripe, or tell God what is wrong when I pray. Prayer, supplication, and thanksgiving are the order of the day. So, I was talking to the **Father,** in the name of **Jesus**, and I knew, that He already knew what we needed. Still, He tells us in His Word to let Him know what we need. After I was done talking to the **Father**, I stepped into the realm of praise and thanksgiving. I lifted my hands and began to dance before the Lord. My dance is not elaborate, orchestrated, symbolic or a performance. It is just me, lifting my feet (kind of kicking them around) and jumping a little bit - in a rather comical, childlike fashion. Some people really believe that they have to get into some kind of elaborate system of swinging their arms and bodies: I just keep it really simple, sincere, and from my heart.

While I was seeking God, my wife was in the kitchen, cleaning up. In the midst of me singing in tongues and dancing before the Lord, there was a knock on the apartment door, which I did not hear. My wife, however, did hear the knocking. She put down the dishes and headed for the door. Now, as far as we were aware, no one knew where we were staying. My wife opened the door to a tall, distinguished-looking, German gentleman. He informed her that he had been looking for us. He said he'd been actually hunting us down, because God had used us in a service where he'd experienced his first supernatural encounter.

My wife came to inform me about the gentleman at the door. So, I walked down the skinny hallway, to where this gentleman was standing, to speak to him. I did have a recollection of meeting him at a previous service; I'd prayed for him to be filled with the Holy Ghost and I remember him speaking in tongues. At the time, I had no idea of his background. He gave me quite an impressive resume of who he was; it turns out he was a professor at a local German college.

He shared with us how he had struggled to believe in the supernatural, because of his superior intellect, but when he came to the service I was ministering at, his world was turned upside down! He had experienced God! When he left that meeting, he said, the Spirit of the Lord was upon him. He also said the Lord spoke to him for the first time he could ever remember. The Lord told him specifically that he was to find me and give me a certain amount of money.

Ever since the Lord had spoken to him (a number of days previously) he had been trying to find us. He had just learned of our address from someone at a church we had been ministering at. Now ... here he was! Standing at our door, during the exact same time when I had been praying—praising and thanking God for the finances and food we needed. Before he left, he handed us an envelope. When he'd gone we opened up the envelope and it was exceedingly abundantly above all that we could ever ask or hope for. We did not have any more financial worries or needs until we left Germany.

#35 Colon Cancer Will Not Kill Me! (2005)

I began to experience some very disturbing symptoms in my body. I will not go into all the details, but there were approximately nine different physical symptoms. One of the symptoms occurred almost every time I had a bowel movement; it looked as if all my innards were coming out. There was blood, green slime, and lots of ugly-looking stuff. During this three month period, I was so sick that sometimes I thought I was going to die at any moment. My normal course of action is that the minute my body begins to manifest any sickness or disease: I immediately command it to go in the Name of Jesus Christ of Nazareth!

But these symptoms simply refused to leave. I made a list of everything that was happening in my body, and I looked the symptoms up on the internet. Every single one of them pointed to colon cancer. I had gone through a similar fight of faith some years previously, with what seemed to be prostate cancer. Once again, I took hold of the Word of God. I boldly declared to the devil, myself, and the spiritual world that I will live and not die. I cried out to Jesus for His mercy and His grace in the midst of this fight of faith. This fight was overwhelming and excruciating at times! Most of my time was spent Praising God, and Thanking Him that I was Healed!

For those three months, I continued with this fight. I spoke to the symptoms and commanded them to go. I kept on praising, thanking and worshiping God, and declaring that I was healed; no ifs, ands or buts. I declared boldly that the devil is a liar! For three months: every day, all day - at times, I declared what God said about me. I did not invite anybody else to stand with me in this fight of faith. Most people, if they'd known what I was going through, would have pronounced me dead and gone. Believe it or not, these are people who call themselves "Christians" and they would have rejoiced in my death. Yes, they would have told people to pray for me - but there would have been more negative comments than the reality of God's Word.

By His stripes we were healed! If I were healed, then I was healed, if I was healed than I am healed. If I am healed then I is healed! For three long months I stood and fought by faith. Many days and nights I walked the floor of our church sanctuary, praising God that I was healed and resisting the spirit of fear. One day, I woke up and all the symptoms had disappeared! Praise God! And they have never come back. Thank you, Jesus!

#36 LESTER SUMRALL OPERATED IN VIOLENT FAITH!

Rev. Dr. Lester Frank Sumrall (February 15, 1913 - April 28, 1996). I had the privilege of knowing Lester. Not only did Lester preach in the church I pastor, but he ordained me as a Minister of the Gospel. I will tell you right now that he was the real McCoy!

I heard a story about Dr. Lester Sumrall some years ago, when he found himself in the middle of the Central American Rainforest. As he went about his ministry in that region, he came across a witch doctor. In today's rock and roll Hollywood scene, this witch doctor would look like a normal man … but, in those days, this was a pretty strange fellow!

In one hand, the witch doctor would hold a bullfrog (always a symbol of satanic power). In the other hand, he held a mixture of human blood and alcohol, and this was placed in the bullfrog's mouth. Then the witch doctor would dance, make satanic incantations and worship demonic entities.

Fortunately, Dr. Sumrall wasn't raised in the modern-day school of humanistic, people-pleasing preachers. All he did was follow Jesus' biblical example and placed his hands on the side of the witch doctor's head, he said two words: **"Come out!"**

The witch doctor fell over with a thud. When he returned to his feet, the witch doctor was born again and started speaking in a heavenly language and glorifying God. Later that night, Dr. Sumrall returned to his room to go to bed. Since it was warm, and without air conditioning, he decided to open the windows while he slept.

As he lay down, a strange odor began to fill the room. Suddenly, all of the sultry heat of the night disappeared from the room. A damp chill filled the place and it was so cold that Dr. Sumrall began to shiver. A wind began to blow the curtains wildly on their rods. Then, the bed began to shake so violently that it moved all the way out into the middle of the floor!

Well, Dr. Sumrall had enough of this! He raised himself up on his bed and said: "You demon spirit, I recognize you. I cast you out earlier today. **In the name of Jesus Christ of Nazareth, you go now!**"

Immediately, the evil presence left the room. The heat returned, the curtains laid down against the wall, the bed stopped shaking and the horrible odor left the room.

Now, most modern-day preachers would have written a book right there! In fact, they would have written seven books: and told how the devil obeyed them. But ... that wasn't Dr. Sumrall's way.

Instead, he rose back up in his bed, looked out of the window and shouted: **"Hey devil! Get back in here!"**

Immediately the curtains began to stick out on end as a wind rushed through the room. The coldness returned ... the smell returned ... the bed began to shake violently and almost shook him out of bed. Dr. Sumrall sat up in his bed and said: "Devil ... When I came into this room, my bed was against that wall. **Now, in the name of Jesus, PUT IT BACK!**"

The bed went shaking back across the room and settled down against the wall. **"Now"** Dr. Sumrall ordered, **"get out of here!"**

Most people will not believe a story like this, but I have personally experienced manifestations of evil spirits in the physical realm. One of the major keys in dealing with devils is that you never glorify them. You never speak highly of them, or exalt them. So many of those who think they are called into the deliverance ministry make a major mistake in this area. It is simply because they do not have faith in God, who created these entities, and He is so much greater than they are – it's no big deal for Him to cast them out.

#37 My Busted, Broken And Bruised Finger Healed! (2009)

We all do stupid things, that is just a part of our humanity. The question is: "Will God still heal us, in spite of our stupidity? I have discovered, many times, that the answer to this question is: "Yes!" Here is another example of something stupid I did ... and God was still there for me.

One day I visited my son, Daniel, at his house. He was in his front room playing a videogame; something called PlayStation

Move, and the game was "Sports Champions." He held a wand in his hand and was thrusting it around and waving it back and forth aggressively. As he was doing this, there was another man on the big screen TV following his moves: a fighting opponent. Right then and there, I should have turned around and walked out … but curiosity got the better of me. He asked if I wanted to play a game with him, because you could have two players at one time fighting each other. I thought about it for a while, and decided, yes I would play. So he handed me another wand and showed me how to activate it. The object of the game was to wave and thrust the sword on the video - by waving the wand in my hand. The man on the screen would follow my movements and fight for me.

He started the game and we began to play. Of course, I had never played this game before, nor do I make a habit of playing video games, so he was winning. I began to get more aggressive trying to win the game, but no matter how much I tried, my son seemed to be able to score points against me. I totally gave in to my flesh and began to wave, stab and wave again my make-believe sword - everywhere. I mean, I really aggressively got into this thing. In the process of trying - with everything inside of me - to win this game I did not notice that I had gotten close to hitting a heavy duty metal case that he had in his front room.

Before I knew what I did, I was sweeping the sword to the right, down and away from me - with all my might; and I slammed my right hand into the corner of the metal cabinet. I am telling you that I really slammed my hand, extremely hard. My son said I hit the cabinet so hard that I dented it! The minute I hit that cabinet, pain exploded through my body. I looked at my index finger and it was all mangled and twisted.

Immediately, it swelled up turning black and blue and it was twisted. Just looking at my busted up index finger made me sick.

I began to jump around, holding my finger with my other hand. And this is what I was crying out to God as I was jumping and screaming: "Lord, please forgive me for being so stupid. Lord, I will never play this game again! I'm so sorry, Father God, in the name of Jesus I repent." I kept jumping around holding onto my finger crying out to God saying: "I repent, I repent, I repent. Forgive me, Lord!"

Daniel looked at my finger and said: "Dad you broke it! You are going to have to go to the doctor." With my finger still full of pain, I told him I did not need a doctor, that I had Jesus Christ and He is the Great Physician. After I made sure that I had sufficient repentance; I spoke to my finger. I commanded my bones to be knit back together and for my finger to be made completely whole. Then I began to thank God that I was healed! I just kept on praising the Lord that my finger was made whole - no matter how it felt or how it looked.

The Spirit of God must have spoken through me, because I told my three sons that by the next morning my finger would be completely well, and they would not be able to tell that I had ever slammed it, by being so stupid. When I was finished making the declaration of faith, I walked away from them holding onto my finger. Even though the pain was throbbing through my body, I just kept thanking God that I was healed.

I went to bed that night and fell asleep holding onto my finger, thanking God that I was healed. I meditated on the Word and confessed that what Jesus did for me, when He had taken the stripes on His back, had the ability to make me completely whole - from any stupid accidents that were my own fault.

The next morning I woke up early to pray and seek God. I had completely forgotten about my finger. Then it hit me … there was no pain! I looked at my index finger and could not even tell that I had busted, broken and bruised it. I was completely healed!! I showed my three sons what God had done for me, in spite of my own stupidity. Daniel still remembers, very vividly, how busted, twisted, broken, black and blue my finger was. I believe that he thinks it was rather funny how I was jumping around, confessing and repenting, and promising God to never do this again.

God is so awesome and amazing! All we have to do is cry out

to Him and He will answer and deliver us from every situation! We simply need to trust in Him, repent, obey Him, and give praise and thanks to Him: no matter how it looks. How long do we keep thanking and praising God? We are to keep knocking and asking until we receive the full manifestation of that which we believe for!

CHAPTER EIGHT

WHAT DO WE NEED TO DO FOR VIOLENT FAITH?

#1 Christ Must Be Exalted Above ALL In Your Heart

Christ was the perfect will of the Heavenly Father manifested and revealed to us in His earthly ministry. We must learn to exalt **Jesus Christ** over all of the afflictions and attacks of the enemy.

Jesus Has ALL Authority And Power In Heaven And Earth!

Matthew 28:18 And Jesus came and spake unto them, saying, All power is given unto me in heaven and in earth.

Colossians 2:15 And having spoiled principalities and powers, he made a shew of them openly, triumphing over them in it.

For this particular truth I will be using the **Book of Hebrews, chapter 1**, and the **Gospel of John, chapter 1**. These two chapters will help you build an amazing foundation for spiritual discernment and casting out devils in every situation. If you embrace what is revealed in these two chapters, your ability to cast out devils will be greatly increased. Let us now take a look at Hebrews, chapter 1.

Hebrews 1:1-3 God, who at sundry times and in divers manners spake in time past unto the fathers by the prophets, 2 Hath in these last days spoken unto us by his Son, whom he hath appointed heir of all things, by whom also he made the worlds; 3 Who being the brightness of his glory, and the express image of his person, and upholding all things by the word of his power, when he had by himself purged our sins, sat down on the right hand of the Majesty on high;

In Hebrews chapter 1, it is revealed that 'in time past' God had spoken to the fathers by the prophets, but, He has now spoken to us by His Son Jesus Christ. According to **Ephesians 2:20 the Kingdom of God is built upon the apostles and prophets; Jesus Christ Himself being the chief cornerstone.** Please notice, that in times past, God spoke specifically by the prophets to the fathers, but now we have a surer word of prophecy; a deeper revelation, and a more precise understanding of the perfect will of our heavenly Father.

Why? Because He is going to speak to us in a very clear and dramatic way. If we believe the words, the life, and the example of Jesus Christ, it will radically transform our lives and the level of **Divine Authority** that we walk in. Remember, all the words and deeds that had been spoken, and revealed, up to the time of Christ, was to prepare us for the **coming of Christ**. The life of Jesus is the perfect will of God manifested in human flesh. This is the mystery which had been hidden before the foundation of the world.

Notice in Hebrews 1:2: *"Hath in these last days spoken unto us by his Son."* The foundation of my understanding of the will of God, the purposes of God, the plans of God, the mission of God and the mysteries of God, cannot be discovered in any greater revelation than the person of Jesus Christ! **There is no greater revelation of God's perfect, divine will or His voice then that which we discover in Jesus Christ.** I cannot emphasize this enough!

If you do not understand that God has revealed Himself to us very precisely, through his son Jesus Christ, you will end up being mixed up, confused, and led astray. Learning the will of God very precisely is only found in **Jesus Christ**, whom He has appointed heir of all things; by whom also He made the worlds. Notice that Hebrews 1:3 boldly declares that Jesus Christ is the brightness of the Father's glory, the manifestation of the Father's presence, and the express image of His personality. Jesus is like a mirror reflecting the perfect image of the heavenly Father to all of humanity. Jesus declared:

John 14:9-10 Jesus saith unto him, Have I been so long time with you, and yet hast thou not known me, Philip? he that hath seen me hath seen the Father; and how sayest thou then, Shew us the Father? 10 Believest thou not that I am in the Father, and the Father in me? the words that I speak unto you I speak not of myself: but the Father that dwelleth in me, he doeth the works.

Jesus Christ is the **absolute perfect will** of the Father revealed to you and me, especially when it comes to healing. The deepest revelation of the Father is only discovered in Jesus Christ! Paul the Apostle commands us to have the mind of Christ.

Philippians 2:5-8 Let this mind be in you, which was also in Christ Jesus: 6 Who, being in the form of God, thought it not robbery to be equal with God: 7 but made himself of no reputation, and took upon him the form of a servant, and was made in the likeness of men: 8 and being found in fashion as a man, he humbled himself, and became obedient unto death, even the death of the cross.

When we look at Jesus, and hear His words, and see His works, it is the Father that we are experiencing. The Apostle John boldly declares this in John 1:

John 1:1-3 IN the beginning was the Word, and the Word was with God, and the Word was God. 2 The same was in the beginning with God. 3 All things were made by him; and without him was not any thing made that was made.

All things were made by the Word. What Word are these Scriptures speaking of? Is it the written Word? Or Christ: The Word? It is obvious that it is talking about the person of Christ Jesus, Emmanuel: God is with us!

John 1:14 And the Word was made flesh, and dwelt among us, (and we beheld his glory, the glory as of the only begotten of the Father,) full of grace and truth.

The reality is that we have to know the person of Christ, discovered in the four Gospels, for us to rightly discern the Word of God. What do I mean by this statement? When I gave my heart to Jesus Christ (February 18, 1975 at about 3 p.m.) all I had available was a little military green Bible. The moment Christ came into my heart, I picked up that little Bible and began to devour it. Matthew, Mark, Luke, and John; the four Gospels of Jesus Christ became my favorite books. I just could not get enough of the wonderful reality of Jesus. As I read the Gospels, I walked with Christ; every step of the way. From His birth, through His childhood, His baptism by John The Baptist when He was thirty-years-old. When He was baptized by the Holy Ghost, and He was led of the Spirit into the wilderness, tempted of the enemy and overcame him by boldly declaring: **"It is written."**

I spent my first three years as a believer eating and drinking nothing but Jesus from the four Gospels. Yes, I did read the epistles, and they were wonderful, but nothing captured and captivated my heart as much as the life, the words, and the ministry of Jesus Christ. I wept as I read of His sufferings, His crucifixion, and His death. I wept when I saw that the Heavenly Father had to turn His face away from His own Son - for our salvation. **I shouted at the triumphant conquest and victory that Jesus had over every satanic power.**

Jesus Christ is the perfect reflection of the Heavenly Father. There is no more perfect revelation of the will of the Father than Jesus Christ. Actually, I am extremely happy that I was not influenced by the modern day church for the first three years of my salvation. When I eventually came to the lower 48, after living and ministering in Alaska, I was shocked and surprised at what most Christians believed. I did not realize that there was such a large variety of different interpretations of the Scriptures in the church. Many of God's people are extremely confused, sick, and defeated; because of a lack of understanding of the will of the Father - revealed to us in the life, ministry and words of Jesus Christ.

Many ministers declare insane false doctrines that are so contrary to what I discovered in **Christ**; it is hard for me to believe that people can even believe what these men are teaching is truth. To truly know the will of God, all you have to do is look at Jesus Christ: His words, deeds, actions, and reactions; His lifestyle and His attitude, mannerisms, His wonderful character, and the fruit of His life. I can truly say that since I have been born again, there is only one person who I truly want to be like: **His name is Jesus Christ**.

If the body of Christ would simply go back to the four Gospels, and walk with Jesus every step of the way: from His birth to His resurrection, to His ascension, much of the confusion would be gone when it comes to the will of God. I believe the reason why so many believers are being deceived by false doctrines, and philosophies, and why they are not receiving their deliverance, is because they do not know, or understand Jesus Christ.

Hebrews 13:8 Jesus Christ the same yesterday, and to day, and forever.

In the old covenant, God says: **"I am the Lord, and I change not."** Without truly seeing the Father, by the words of Jesus Christ, and by the life of Jesus Christ, you can easily be led astray by crafty men misusing the Scriptures. You have to see Jesus to understand not just the Old Testament, but also the epistles of the New Testament. Jesus is the voice of God; the absolute perfect will of the Father, the manifestation of God on Earth.

I have heard ministers use the Bible to contradict the teachings of Jesus Christ. The reason why false doctrines have been able to take root in the church is because people have not looked and listened to Jesus in the four Gospels. If, in your mind and heart, you exalt Christ and His teaching - above all else - it will be very difficult for the enemy to lead you astray with false teachings and doctrines.

Matthew 9:33 And when the devil was cast out, the dumb spake: and the multitudes marvelled, saying, It was never so seen in Israel.

Matthew 10:1 And when he had called unto him his twelve disciples, he gave them power against unclean spirits, to cast them out, and to heal all manner of sickness and all manner of disease.

Matthew 10:8 Heal the sick, cleanse the lepers, raise the dead, cast out devils: freely ye have received, freely give.

Matthew 12:28 But if I cast out devils by the Spirit of God, then the kingdom of God is come unto you.

Mark 16:17 And these signs shall follow them that believe; In my name shall they cast out devils; they shall speak with new tongues;

Luke 11:20 But if I with the finger of God cast out devils, no doubt the kingdom of God is come upon you.

Luke 10:19 Behold, I give unto you power to tread on serpents and scorpions, and over all the power of the enemy: and nothing shall by any means hurt you.

Luke 9:42 And as he was yet a coming, the devil threw him down, and tare him. And Jesus rebuked the unclean spirit, and healed the child, and delivered him again to his father.

Luke 4:36 And they were all amazed, and spake among themselves, saying, What a word is this! for with authority and power he commandeth the unclean spirits, and they come out.

Luke 6:18 And they that were vexed with unclean spirits: and they were healed.

#2 Operate In The Realm Of Faith!

The second principle, or step, in Moving in Strong Faith is that you must get into the realm of faith. Jesus taught more on the subject of faith (in the four Gospels) than any other subject. This place, this dimension, this world that we call **FAITH** is beyond the human equation, or understanding. This goes way beyond the intellect, feelings, emotions, and the circumstances of life.

*Isaiah 55:8-9 For my thoughts are not your thoughts, neither are your ways my ways, saith the Lord. 9 For as the heavens are higher than the earth, so are my ways higher than your ways, and my thoughts than your thoughts.

In order to get into this reality of **Faith**, it must be accomplished by way of the Word of God. The Bible says that natural men did not dream up **the Bible**, but spoke, and wrote as God moved upon them.

*2 Peter 1:21 For the prophecy came not in old time by the will of man: but holy men of God spake as they were moved by the

Holy Ghost.

In Hebrews, chapter 11, we see amazing miracles, signs, and wonders, all accomplished by faith: by men and women just like you and I. In the Old Testament, and in the New Testament, and all the way to the end of the Bible, people lived and moved by faith. The only way to get into this world, realm, and place of **Faith -** where all things are possible - is by unwavering trust and confidence in God and His Word. Everything that I share with you in this book is to help bring you into this place of **Faith.** Without faith, it is impossible to please God.

*Hebrews 11:6 But without faith it is impossible to please him: for he that cometh to God must believe that he is, and that he is a rewarder of them that diligently seek him.

Faith Is Like A Diamond With Many Facets And Yet It Is The Same Diamond!

Faith is spoken of in a very strong way (belief and trust) over eight-hundred times in the Bible! **Jesus** did more teaching on the subject of faith than on any other subject. I cannot overemphasize the importance of having faith in Christ to Operate in Authority and Power! Before we go any further, I need to explain what I mean when I say "faith." As I read the Word of God I discover there is *only one true faith*, that is faith in **CHRIST JESUS**! All other faiths and beliefs - no matter what you may call them - according to the Word of God, they are not faith at all! It may be a belief system or a psychological philosophy: but it is not faith!

When Christ ascended up on high, He gave gifts unto men: He gave some apostles, some prophets, some evangelist, pastors and teachers. Now, these men and women need to be walking in the **Realm of Faith.** If they are not walking in faith, they cannot bring you into faith. If they are not walking in **obedience**, they cannot bring you into a place of **obedience**. If they are not walking in deliverance and freedom, they cannot bring you into that place.

Now, if we as ministers are not submitted to Christ, how can we bring you into that realm of **Submission**? These fivefold ministry gifts that Christ gave should be, and need to be, walking in this realm of faith. I'm not discrediting these men and women if they are not walking there, but it will be very difficult for these ministry gifts to help you receive what God has for you, if they are not walking in it themselves. Basically, we take people to the place where we're at.

Hebrews 11 gives us a description of faith and its manifestations. Let's look very briefly at Hebrews 11:1-3.

Hebrews 11:1-3 <u>NOW faith</u> is the <u>substance</u> of things hoped for, the <u>evidence</u> of things not seen. 2 For by it the elders obtained a good report. 3 Through <u>faith</u> we understand that the worlds were framed by the word of God, so that things which are seen were not made of things which do appear.

So, we can boldly declare that faith is a substance - that gives evidence - by which "the worlds were framed by the word of God." Only the Christian faith (faith in **CHRIST JESUS**) is what brought about, and continues to sustain creation and all that exists. It is very important for us to understand that there is **only one faith**! This faith is the **only faith** that saves, heals, delivers, creates, pleases God, and makes all things possible!

Ephesians 4:4-6 There is one body, and one Spirit, even as ye are called in one hope of your calling; 5 One Lord, <u>one faith</u>, one baptism, 6 One God and Father of all, who is above all, and through all, and in you all.

Did you hear that? There is only **one true faith**, and that is faith in **CHRIST JESUS**! There is no other name under heaven, given among men, whereby we must be saved, healed, delivered, set free, and transformed! **TRUE FAITH** always takes dominion over the world, the flesh, and the devil! Faith in **Christ** always produces positive results and brings victory: in every situation! Many people are operating in presumption, natural reasoning, mental acknowledgment, and yet they truly believe that they are operating in faith (In **Christ Jesus**). The truth of the matter is --- **they are not!**

1 John 5:3-5 For this is the love of God, that we keep his commandments: and his commandments are not grievous. 4 For whatsoever is born of God overcometh the world: and this is the victory that overcometh the world, even our faith. 5 Who is he that overcometh the world, but he that believeth that Jesus is the Son of God?

Every human being, when they were conceived within their mother's womb, was invested with the divine seed of faith. It is extremely important that **we acknowledge this reality** so that we do not allow our enemy (the devil) to deceive us into believing that we have no faith. Not only were we created with faith, but we were created by faith, by **Christ Jesus, God the Father, and the Holy Ghost!**

John 1:3 *All things were made by him; and without him was not any thing made that was made.*

Let's take a look at Scriptures taken from the Book of Genesis:

Genesis 1:26-27 And God said, Let us make man in our <u>image</u>, after our likeness: and let them have dominion over the fish of the sea, and over the fowl of the air, and over the cattle, and over all the earth, and over every creeping thing that creepeth upon the earth. 27 So God created man in his own <u>image</u>, in the image of God created he him; male and female created he them.

Did you notice that man was created in the image of God! How does God operate and function? We could talk about the character of God; dealing with His love, mercy, forgiveness, long-suffering, gentleness, kindness, meekness, holiness, faithfulness, joy, goodness, and many other attributes; but all of these spring from the fact that He operates in faith. There is a very interesting Scripture that declares this, found in the book of Timothy:

2 Timothy 2:13 If we believe not, yet he abideth faithful: he cannot deny himself. And in Romans it declares..........

Romans 3:3 For what if some did not believe? shall their unbelief make the faith of God without effect?

All of creation is sustained, maintained, and consists upon the reality of God having faith in **Himself**. We were created and made to walk in that realm of faith, by trusting and having confidence, total reliance, complete dependence upon nothing but God. The only way the enemy could defeat man was by getting him out of the arena of faith. He had to sow the seed of unbelief into the soil of man's heart. Adam and Eve took the bait, thereby stepping out of the realm of faith: into a nightmare of death, poverty, fear, hate, lust, disobedience, sickness, and disease.

A Pandora's Box Had Been Opened!

Christ Jesus came to shut that box, by bringing men back into a position of absolute and total faith, confidence, trust, obedience and dependence upon God. Let's look at John 1:9 because within it is the evidence that at our conception God gave us faith:

John 1:9 That was the true Light, which lighteth <u>every man</u> that cometh into the world.

This light which "lighteth" up every man that comes into the world is the seed of faith, trust, and confidence in God. **Jesus** boldly declared that to enter into the kingdom of heaven, we must have the faith of a child! Everything that **Jesus** ever spoke was absolute truth. There was no exaggeration in anything He declared.

Everything he spoke is the absolute, complete, and total truth. We can, and must, base our life totally upon what He declared!

Matthew 18:3 And said, Verily I say unto you, Except ye be converted, and become as little children, ye shall not enter into the kingdom of heaven.

Mark 10:15 Verily I say unto you, Whosoever shall not receive the kingdom of God as a little child, he shall not enter therein.

Luke 18:17 Verily I say unto you, Whosoever shall not receive the kingdom of God as a little child shall in no wise enter therein.

Jesus was declaring that unless you once again have the **faith of a little child** (this is true conversion) you will never be able to enter in! We could look at all the attributes of a little child, which I believe is a natural manifestation of true faith in **Christ**! If you believe the Scripture I am about to share; it will clear up much confusion when it comes to those who have **not heard** the gospel. Please understand, faith simply takes God at His Word without any argument or doubting.

Romans 1:20-21 For the invisible things of him from the creation of the world are clearly seen, being understood by the things that are made, even his eternal power and Godhead; so that they are without excuse: 21 Because that, when they knew God, they glorified him not as God, neither were thankful; but became vain in their imaginations, and their foolish heart was darkened.

Did you notice that it says man is without excuse? Because, at some time he understood? I know this sounds extremely strange, but, it's true! Well, how would a child understand? Part of this mystery can be answered by Hebrews 11:3:

Hebrews 11:3 Through faith we understand that the worlds were framed by the word of God, so that things which are seen were not made of things which do appear.

When faith is alive and active, it understands, not with human reasoning, but from the inner-depths of the heart. At the conception of every human being there was an invisible substance called faith. Now, the day comes when a person knowingly, and willingly goes against the faith that is in his heart, thereby entering into a condition of what God calls "death." Death is when we no longer have a pure, and holy faith in God out of the sincerity of our heart. It is when we willingly, and knowingly break the laws of God.

Remember when Mary told Elizabeth (her aunt) that she was having a baby … and that this baby was the Son of God? What took place at that moment? The Bible tells us that the baby within Elizabeth's womb (John The Baptist) leaped for joy! What caused this excitement in the heart of the unborn child? He was **full of faith**. He understood, even in his mother's womb, that **Jesus** was the Son of God, the Lamb of God and that He had come to the Earth. This brought tremendous joy to his heart. This is another reason why he could be filled with the Spirit from his mother's womb, because the Holy Ghost dwells in the atmosphere of faith.

Romans 7:9 For I was alive without the law once: but when the commandment came, sin revived, and I died.

Jesus Christ came to resurrect, within the heart of every man, **complete and absolute faith, trust, confidence, dependence, reliance, and obedience to God the Father**! Do not allow the enemy to tell you that you were born without faith. Faith is your natural habitat and dwelling place; just like the birds in the air, and the fish in the sea. Step back into your rightful position!

It is important for us to understand that when we are born into this world, every part of our existence still needs to be developed. Whether it be our bones, muscles, organs, even our thinking and reasoning processes. **Even so, it is with Faith**. Our faith must be developed, grow and become strong. This particular book deals with the subject of healing, but I have written other books dealing with the subject of faith. One such book is: "How Faith Comes: 28 Ways That FAITH Comes" which deals with how your faith can grow, mature and be developed in 28 ways! I strongly encourage you to purchase this book at Amazon: it is available for free, or only $0.99 as a Kindle book, or e-book.

#3 Eat & Drink The Word

The Bible says that in the last days, there is going to be a famine in the land. In my opinion, the famine has already manifested: it is a famine of God's Word hidden in the heart of believers. Many believers do not understand God. They do not know how to trust God, or how to look to God, because there has been a lack in leadership of those who move in the realm of faith and the Word. Many modern church leaders are successful not because of faith in **Christ, and God's Word**, but simply because they are worldly-wise. They use natural, practical, worldly wisdom to grow their local churches; and yet Scripture declares: *Matthew 4:4: "It is written, Man shall not live by bread alone, but by every word that proceedeth out of the mouth of God."*

MOST OF THE PEOPLE THAT WE CALL 'SUCCESSFUL PASTORS' ARE SIMPLY WORLDLY-WISE MEN. TRUE SUCCESS IS WHEN WE SEE THE IMAGE & CHARACTER OF CHRIST BEING FORMED IN PEOPLE!

Proverbs 3:5-6 Trust in the Lord with all thine heart; and lean not unto thine own understanding. In all thy ways acknowledge him, and he shall direct thy paths.

If you read Hebrews 11, there are fifty events in this particular chapter! We call this chapter the "Faith Hall of Fame." We need to take a really good look at these men and women: the conditions they were experiencing; and how they responded to all of the trials, tribulations, and tests. They overcame **by faith: based upon the Word that God** had given to them. It is a faith that works by love, and when you walk in this realm of faith: you will not worry; you will not be fearful; you will not be angry; you will not be frustrated; you will not be upset; you will not be self-centered; you will not be self-serving and self-seeking; and you will not be self-pleasing.

True Biblical Faith takes a hold of God's Word, and the divine nature of **Christ,** and will not let go. When **Jesus** said faith made a person whole, what He was saying is: "Your confidence in Me, My Word, and in **My Father** has made you whole." Therefore, it is faith in **these three areas** that make all things possible! The **third step, realm, or reality, that must be in our life to bring deliverance** is that we must eat and drink the **Word of God**. We must eat and drink the words of Christ, even as the descendants of Abraham partook of the Passover Lamb.

John 6:1-4 After these things Jesus went over the sea of Galilee, which is the sea of Tiberias. 2 And a great multitude followed him, because they saw his miracles which he did on them that were diseased. 3 And Jesus went up into a mountain, and there he sat with his disciples. 4 And the passover, a feast of the Jews, was nigh.

The **Passover** is indeed the most important festival, feast day, tradition and ceremony of the Jewish people. To better comprehend what the **Passover** is, we'll have to step back into history, and take a look in the biblical Book of Exodus; when God sent Moses to deliver the Israelites from the hands of Pharaoh.

The Israelites had been in captivity for four-hundred years before God sent Moses to bring deliverance and freedom to them. Of course, Moses is a typology of **Jesus Christ**, who came to set us free from the slavery of sin, by, or through, the means of us having faith in **Christ and His Word**. God told Pharaoh, through Moses, to let His people go. We all know the story of how Pharaoh refused to obey God. The Lord had Moses bring plague after plague to free His people from the hands of Pharaoh. None of the plagues convinced Pharaoh to loose God's people, so there was to be one last judgment: the **Passover lamb**. This would be the final blow to Egypt and would release the children of God. By and through the **Passover** God would change the world. From that moment forward nothing would ever be the same.

As you and I receive revelation on the **Passover**, and what it means to us, our lives will never be the same. In the Bible, the **Passover** is mentioned **seventy-three times**! Furthermore, the **lamb**, or the **Passover lamb, is mentioned one-hundred times!** As a result of the **Passover**, the children of Israel, from that day forward (if they believed the words of Moses) could walk in health, and receive divine healing.

Psalm 105:37 He brought them forth also with silver and gold: and there was not one feeble person among their tribes.

Exodus 15:26 And said, If thou wilt diligently hearken to the voice of the Lord thy God, and wilt do that which is right in his sight, and wilt give ear to his commandments, and keep all his statutes, I will put none of these diseases upon thee, which I have brought upon the Egyptians: for I am the LORD that healeth thee.

Did you notice that God told Moses everyone should take a lamb without spot or blemish? The Lord also told Moses that if they obey Him in the keeping of this celebration, it will finally set them **free from the control of the enemy**! If we, as believers, would do likewise, with the revelation of **Christ** our **Passover lamb**, we would truly be set free; and set others free!

What is the **Third Step** in our preparation in setting people free?

Eating & Drinking Jesus Christ and the Word of God!

Hebrews 11:28 Through faith he kept the passover, and the sprinkling of blood, lest he that destroyed the firstborn should touch them.

Audacious, Violent Faith comes when you eat of the **Passover** using God's **WORD** with a sincere heart of love and devotion. Of course, the **Passover lamb** is **Jesus Christ**, the only begotten Son of God. John the Baptist had a revelation of **Jesus Christ** when he was baptizing at the river Jordan. He saw **Jesus** walk towards him and said: **"Behold the Lamb of God Which Taketh Away The Sin of the World!"** (John 1:29).

There were certain conditions that had to be met, so the people had a right to partake of the **Passover lamb**, and to protect them from the Death Angel that was going to pass through the land. Everyone must be dressed ready to leave; the **blood of the lamb** had to be applied to the door post and lintel - which is symbolic of our thought life and the works of the flesh. Plus, all of the men had to be physically circumcised.

To do the **Passover** justice, we would have to look at every spiritual truth and every lesson that is wrapped up in the **Passover:** which, in itself could easily be a book. Suffice it to say, as we partake of the bread and the grape juice, as **Jesus** commanded us; and recognize by faith that it is His body and His blood which He gave for our salvation; faith will begin to rise in our hearts for our deliverance, and the deliverance of others.

In the Garden of Gethsemane **Jesus** prayed to His Father: *"if it be possible, let this cup pass from me: nevertheless not as I will, but as thou wilt" Matthew 26:39*. The cup He was speaking of was the cup of cursing. The old covenant mentions the curse placed upon sinful flesh: **Jesus Christ** became a curse for us so that we might be made free from the curse of the law. Everyone that speaks the name of **Christ** is required to keep the **Passover**. Exodus 12:47 says: *"All the congregation of Israel shall keep it."* However, I am not referring to the one observed in Exodus, but rather what **Christ** declares today:

John 6:48-51 & 55-57 I am that bread of life. 49 Your fathers did eat manna in the wilderness and are dead. 50 This is the bread which cometh down from heaven, that a man may eat thereof, and not die. 51 I am the living bread which came down from heaven: if any man eats of this bread, he shall live for ever: and the bread that I will give is my flesh, which I will give for the life of the world...... 55 For my flesh is meat indeed, and my blood is drink indeed. 56 He that eateth my flesh, and drinketh my blood, dwelleth in me, and I in him. 57 As the living Father hath sent me, and I live by the Father: so he that eateth me, even he shall live by me.

As we develop intimacy with **Christ,** we come into a oneness with **Jesus Christ and His Word.** We can never overemphasize the need to apprehend, and develop our faith in **Christ.** The growth, development, and increase of our faith is extremely important to our success in bringing **FREEDOM** to all those we minister to. Everything we have, and everything we partake of, in **Christ,** has to be done by faith. All things were created by God: by faith. God created all things by having faith in Himself! True believers are those who do not trust in themselves; but trust in God and have faith in God.

Psalm 37:5 Commit thy way unto the Lord; trust also in him; and he shall bring it to pass.

Jesus asked if at the very end of the ages, right before He returns, would be there any faith left on the earth? The faith we are talking about here is a faith that apprehends the character, nature, the mind, the heart, and the will of God. A faith that takes a hold of **Jesus Christ,** and brings the believer into a place of victory: over sin, the world, the flesh, sickness, disease, infirmities, and the devil.

Faith is like the physical muscles in your body. Many people are physically out of shape in America. It is not because we have fewer muscles than previous generations. We have the same muscles that our parents, grandparents, or even our great-great-grandparents had. Most people are simply out of shape because they are not exercising their natural muscles. Neither are they eating the proper type of foods. The natural world is symbolic of what's going on in the spiritual world: spiritually, people are not exercising their faith, and they are not eating the proper spiritual foods.

#38 Dangerous Attack Of Conjunctivitis (1993)

I am sharing this story to help you understand how to take a hold of your healing. The minute any type of physical affliction attacks your body is the very moment you need to take a hold of God's Word and come against the enemy of your soul. Your body is the temple of the Holy Ghost, and the enemy has no right to afflict it!

John 10:10 The thief cometh not, but for to steal, and to kill, and to destroy.

James 4:7 Submit yourselves therefore to God. Resist the devil, and he will flee from you.

A brother from the church I pastor had accompanied me to the Philippines. We were ministering in the province of Samar, which is one of the five provinces of the Philippines. It takes an airplane ride from Manila, and then a transfer to ground vehicles. The trip is rather long, tiring and challenging. Not including the fact that we were in the territory of the New People's Army, which is an anti-government communist movement. Believe me when I say they would kill you in a heartbeat.

So, when we finally arrived at our destination, the Filipinos that we would be working with were waiting for us. The local pastors, and believers, had already prepared the way for us to hold crusades in different towns and villages. In the natural, they really did not need us, because they were all walking in the realities of God. To some extent, we Americans were like White Elephants in that we drew a crowd. However, we did not have any more of the Holy Spirit or the Word of God than they did.

As we made our way to the first set of meetings, all of our team, including myself, were attacked with conjunctivitis, commonly called: "Pinkeye." Conjunctivitis is caused by a virus that can be dangerous in two ways: Firstly, the person with the infection can lose some of their vision - in severe cases they can totally lose their eyesight - this could be for a short time, or it could be permanent. Secondly, the infection can spread very rapidly, and is highly infectious. People with "Pinkeye" often get conjunctivitis germs on their hands by rubbing their eyes, then leave germs on objects they touch.

The first sign of this affliction is that your eyes begin to feel dry and irritated. Then it gets to the point where it literally feels like someone has grabbed a handful of sand and shoved it into your eyes; grinding your eyeballs slowly with the sand. The whites of your eyes eventually turn pink, and can become blood-red when it's really bad.

The minute my eyes started to feel irritated, I found a quiet place of prayer. I simply spoke to my heavenly Father and thanked Him for what Jesus had done for me when He received the stripes upon His back. After meditating upon this for a short while, it was time to take the authority that Christ has given to all believers. I spoke to this affliction in the name of Jesus, commanding it to go: Now! Now! Now! In the name of Jesus Christ of Nazareth! No ifs, ands or buts. I followed with thanksgiving and praise - I thanked God that I was healed. Not that I was going to be healed, but, that I was healed already! From that moment forward it did not matter how I felt, or looked. I knew that I knew that I knew that I was healed. I just kept on thanking and praising God, quietly, and in my heart.

I went on my way – rejoicing! Even though I did not feel any different, or look any different. Not one more word came out of my mouth about this affliction; or how terrible my eyes felt. Within less than two days all of the symptoms were gone!

I'm sorry to say that this was not the case for the rest of the team. A lot of these precious people were going through terrible irritation. The brother I had brought with me began to get much worse. Eventually the whites of his eyes turned blood-red. I knew in my heart that if we did not do something he could go blind. This continued for over a week; then he finally told me that he had to get back to America. I learned a long time ago not to be critical of people, but to work with them - where they are at. He told me that I could continue with the meetings - but he was leaving! I informed everyone that I would travel back to America with this brother and make sure he got back home. He was my responsibility; I was his pastor and also the spiritual authority of these meetings.

Of course, my precious Filipino brothers were slightly upset and disappointed, because there were meetings that still needed to be fulfilled. I informed them that I was sorry, but my first responsibility was to this brother, and the Holy Ghost would move through them, and speak through them.

In order to cut our trip short, it was going to take faith to get on the plane earlier than we were scheduled to leave. And we also had to believe that we were not going to be stopped by customs because of the highly contagious affliction in his eyes. All the way home he wore dark sunglasses. Through a series of miracles, we were able to board a plane early and get back to America.

The infection he had picked up in the Philippines did not leave him, without medical help. Thank God he did not lose his eyesight. Jesus always works with us - where we are at. My position is one of being there for people, no matter what. We help, pray and encourage where we can. If we do not see a miracle, we simply keep our eyes on Jesus. If we fall short, we just determine in our heart to get back up and keep on going. If I run into situations where it does not seem like I can receive healing, I just go deeper into God, His Word, and His will for my life. God will never let you down!

Violent Faith Is Revealed To Us Throughout The Scriptures!

I encourage you to look up the following biblical characters to see **Violent, Aggressive, Radical Faith** in action:

#1 Enoch
#2 Noah
#3 Abraham
#4 Jacob
#5 Joseph
#6 Moses
#7 Joshua
#8 Caleb
#9 Samuel
#10 David
#11 Elijah
#12 Elisha
#13 Prophets of Old

New Testament:
#1 Jesus Christ
#2 Peter
#3 John
#4 Blind Bartimaeus
#5 Phoenician woman
#6 Woman with the issue of blood
#7 Zacchaeus
#8 Centurion
#9 Paul
#10 Stephen
#11 Barnabas
#12 Philip
#13 Many Saints of the New Testament

CHAPTER NINE

#4. Be Extremely Serious

The fourth step in setting people free is: You must become very serious about helping people. You must even go beyond "serious" to the place of truly meaning business or you could say: **get to the point of being desperate**. Yes, you must become desperate to set others free: desperate to bring deliverance and desperate to see people made whole.

The Bible says the kingdom of heaven suffers violence, and the violent take it by force.

I want you to know that you **MUST** be serious! You have to mean business! The major problem is that many Christians take the pathway of least resistance. It is just so easy to run to the world and get worldly help; and it is very easy to run to the doctors and trust in the arm of the flesh. Please do not misunderstand me with the statements I am making. Truly, I am not attacking people who use the world, I'm simply stating that in the midst of running to the world, instead of looking to God, we are tying the hands of God, and cutting ourselves off from a Miracle. There are many Scriptures that deal with not trusting in God, and trusting man instead.

Jeremiah 17:5 Thus saith the LORD; Cursed be the man that trusteth in man, and maketh flesh his arm, and whose heart departeth from the Lord.

Psalm 118:8-9 It is better to trust in the LORD than to put confidence in man. 9 It is better to trust in the LORD than to put confidence in princes.

Isaiah 2:22 Cease ye from man, whose breath is in his nostrils: for wherein is he to be accounted of ?

Psalm 146:3-4 Put not your trust in princes, nor in the son of man, in whom there is no help. 4 His breath goeth forth, he returneth to his earth; in that very day his thoughts perish.

Isaiah 31:1 Woe to them that go down to Egypt for help; and stay on horses, and trust in chariots, because they are many; and in horsemen, because they are very strong, but they look not unto the Holy One of Israel, neither seek the LORD!

God wants us to trust Him! God wants us to come to Him! God wants to help us! God wants us to believe Him! But … He is not going to make you. The **fourth step** you must take is that you have to become serious. Very Serious! You could even say desperate when it comes to God using you. **Pacifism** will open the door for the devil: possibly even killing you when it comes to casting out devils. There is no room for pacifism in this fight of faith: *"For we wrestle not against flesh and blood, but against principalities, against powers, against the rulers of the darkness of this world, against spiritual wickedness in high places" Ephesians 6:12.* The thief, the devil, has come to steal, to kill, and to destroy you.

Acts 10:38 How God anointed Jesus of Nazareth with the Holy Ghost and with power: who went about doing good, and healing all that were oppressed of the devil; for God was with him.

We see many illustrations throughout the Scriptures of people who are serious about being free, delivered, and healed; and God did not disappoint even one of them! In the Book of Revelation, when Christ was speaking to the church, He said He was not happy with them because they were "lukewarm." They were lackadaisical, laid back, taking it easy pacifists. He said because they were neither cold, nor hot, but because they were lukewarm He would vomit them out of His mouth. As long as you are lukewarm in your attitude towards your healing, it will be very difficult for you to receive your miracle. I strongly encourage you to read the following three accounts from the Gospels.

The first account is of the woman with the issue of blood; who pressed her way through the masses to be healed by Jesus Christ:

Matthew 9:20-22 And, behold, a woman, which was diseased with an issue of blood twelve years, came behind him, and touched the hem of his garment: 21 For she said within herself, If I may but touch his garment, I shall be whole. 22 But Jesus turned him about, and when he saw her, he said, Daughter, be of good comfort; thy faith hath made thee whole. And the woman was made whole from that hour.

The second account is of the blind man, Bartimaeus. Even with the disciples of Jesus telling him to be quiet, he would not shut up until he received from Christ that which he believed for:

Mark 10:46-52 And they came to Jericho: and as he went out of Jericho with his disciples and a great number of people, blind Bartimaeus, the son of Timaeus, sat by the highway side begging. 47 And when he heard that it was Jesus of Nazareth, he began to cry out, and say, Jesus, thou son of David, have mercy on me. 48 And many charged him that he should hold his peace: but he cried the more a great deal, Thou son of David, have mercy on me. 49 And Jesus stood still and commanded him to be called. And they call the blind man, saying unto him, Be of good comfort, rise; he calleth thee. 50 And he, casting away his garment, rose, and came to Jesus. 51 And Jesus answered and said unto him, What wilt thou that I should do unto thee? The blind man said unto him, Lord, that I might receive my sight. 52 And Jesus said unto him, Go thy way; thy faith hath made thee whole. And immediately he received his sight, and followed Jesus in the way.

The third account is of a **Phoenician woman whose daughter needed to be delivered from demons**. In this particular situation, it appears that Jesus spoke words that were very offensive. The woman did not allow this to discourage her, but pressed in until Jesus answered her prayers: and **her daughter was delivered**. This is so vitally important when it comes to us receiving our healing, which Christ has already purchased for us.

Matthew 15:21-28 Then Jesus went thence, and departed into the coasts of Tyre and Sidon. 22 And, behold, a woman of Canaan came out of the same coasts, and cried unto him, saying, Have mercy on me, O Lord, thou son of David; my daughter is grievously vexed with a devil. 23 But he answered her not a word. And his disciples came and besought him, saying, Send her away; for she crieth after us. 24 But he answered and said, I am not sent but unto the lost sheep of the house of Israel. 25 Then came she and worshipped him, saying, Lord, help me. 26 But he answered and said, It is not meet to take the children's bread, and to cast it to dogs. 27 And she said, Truth, Lord: yet the dogs eat of the crumbs which fall from their masters' table. 28 Then Jesus answered and said unto her, O woman, great is thy faith: be it unto thee even as thou wilt. And her daughter was made whole from that very hour.

This is the **mystery of active and living faith in Christ** being manifested in a person's life. If you are serious and desperate, you will be a be a 'doer' of taking a hold of God and not letting go. Even in the world, success is only achieved by those who are truly serious about what they are involved in. It is God's will to bring deliverance to you, and healing to you: but it will take **violent faith**. I have run into many believers who have a twisted, perverted view when it comes to **TRUSTING GOD**. They get caught up in weird, mystical methods! I hope you realize that the salvation and freedom which **Christ** has purchased for us was not easily accomplished, or cheaply bought. When Jesus said:

John 14:12 Verily, verily, I say unto you, He that believeth on me, the works that I do shall he do also; and greater works than these shall he do; because I go unto my Father.

The works He was referring to was the aggressive, violent, and desperate acts of faith that He accomplished with Him even going all the way to the whipping post, the cross, and the grave. He had determined in His heart that He would obey the Father in all that He was asked to do: until its ultimate conclusion.

Isaiah 50:7 For the Lord God will help me; therefore shall I not be confounded: therefore have I set my face like a flint, and I know that I shall not be ashamed.

In the last forty years I have seen many people set free by **aggressively taking a hold of God, and not letting go**. You have to take the bull by the horns, put the axe to the grinding wheel and make the dust fly if you are going to set people free. I am amazed at what people are willing to allow the medical world to do to them so that they might be made whole. If we would only turn all of this desperation, this **overwhelming seriousness** towards the Lord, I believe we would see many more miracles, deliverances and healings in our lives. God gave the children of Israel the land that flowed with milk and honey, but did you notice that they had to fight for it? The Apostle Paul said: *2 Timothy 4:7: "I have fought a good fight, I have finished my course, I have kept the faith:"*

There must be a faith in your heart that rises and takes a hold of God's promises when it comes to divine healing.

For over forty years now, I have aggressively, violently, and persistently taken a hold of Gods will. I refuse to let the devil rob me of what Jesus so painfully purchased. It is mine! The devil cannot have it. The thought never even enters my mind to see a doctor when physical sickness attacks my body. You see, I already have a doctor, and His name is **Jesus Christ of Nazareth**. He is the Great Physician, and He has already healed me with His stripes. Yes, there have been times when the manifestation of my healing seemed like it would never come ... but I knew, that I knew, that I knew by His stripes I am healed. Strong faith never considers the circumstances.

#5 Never Exalt The Devil!

The fifth step of God using you to bring deliverance, or be delivered, is that you **must never, never, ever** exalt the devil, or evil manifestations, or negative circumstances or any symptoms in a victim. **What do I mean by this statement?** I hear many Christians exalting the devil or their problems, and yet, I have personally known believers that had major problems, but never talked about them, never made a big deal out of them, and never even told people what they were going through.

We need to see people rise up in **faith**, and go after the **will of God**. When faith is in operation, it will cause you to pray, gather together with the Saints, meditate upon Gods Word, deny your flesh, share your faith and testimony with others, and take care of the needy. In America, we have lost our faith in **Christ**, and yet there is still great hope; because our faith can be restored in **Christ**. God desires us to have great faith to bring deliverance, and He has provided for us many different ways to acquire it. All of these blessings, provisions and protections will be activated in our lives as we are **dwelling** and **abiding** in **Jesus**.

2 Timothy 1:7 For God hath not given us the spirit of fear; but of power, and of love, and of a sound mind.

There's no fear of what man can do to you, or of any sickness, disease, poverty, financial lack, plagues, afflictions, or demonic spirits. There's no fear; there's no worry, and there's no torment when we are walking in the realm of faith, based upon the will, and the Word of God. You will have a peace that surpasses all understanding, joy unspeakable, and you will be full of glory. When someone is sick in the natural we can put our hands on their forehead to see if they are running a fever. The doctor can have you open your mouth, and take a look at your tonsils, or your tongue. Symptoms in your physical body will reveal sickness by certain manifestations. This is also true when it comes to divine faith. If you are truly operating in faith, the divine attributes of **Christ** will be manifested. The nine fruits of the spirit should be evident. You will be living a holy, separated, consecrated life for God. If you are not, then it is evidence that you need to step back into that realm of faith: by eating and drinking Jesus Christ, and meditating upon God's Word.

One time, when Smith Wigglesworth (an amazing man of Faith) had a real serious financial situation, he went to pray for a wealthy man. When Smith prayed for this wealthy man, the man was gloriously healed and delivered right then and there! The wealthy man told Smith that he wanted to bless him, and asked if there was anything he could do to help him? Smith replied: "No brother" but thanked him anyway for the offer. Smith was looking to God to take care of a desperate financial need. By the way, God did do an amazing miracle to meet this financial need!

#39 "God Shall Operate"

On another occasion, Smith Wigglesworth ended up with a terrible affliction of gallstones. He was informed by a specialist that the only way to deliver him from the gallstones was by an operation. Smith's son-in-law, James Salter, said that during the whole three years of this trial, Smith never stopped preaching, never complained, or told anyone. Even though Smith Wigglesworth was in great pain, and bled a great deal, he continued to minister to the sick, even with **blood running down his legs**, filling his socks and shoes, as he laid hands on the sick. He did end up spending many days in bed, in great pain, but he would get up to make it to the meetings where he was to minister. This test went on day, after day, after another day, and night, after night.

It is reported that the meetings he conducted during this time were powerful, with many attesting to the wonderful miracles of God's healing power. When deliverance finally manifested in Smith's body, it was almost instantaneous; with all twenty-plus gallstones removed. Smith Wigglesworth was made completely and perfectly whole. Smith put those stones in a small tin can and on occasions he would show the stones to different people as he told them of Gods faithfulness.

Some of the stones were quite large: others were jagged and needle shaped. All of the stones not only caused tremendous pain but penetrated his innards in such a way that it caused constant hemorrhaging. Smith was a man who understood what it meant to have faith, and he worked by patience. He had an unshakable faith that caused him to agree with God, and to disagree with the circumstances - no matter the pain, or problem.

Whenever we exalt the devil through sickness, or the afflictions or problems of our lives, we are operating in a spirit of unbelief. I am not saying that we cannot share privately, with people of faith, what we are going through, so that they can agree and believe with us. In over forty years of walking with Christ, I have shared very little with people of what I was being confronted with. I knew that most people were not truly going to be believing with me, but would simply tell others what I was going through. I'd like to share an example of this with you, taken from the ministry of Jesus: the father who had a demon-possessed son.

Mark 9:17-27 And one of the multitude answered and said, Master, I have brought unto thee my son, which hath a dumb spirit; 18 And wheresoever he taketh him, he teareth him: and he foameth, and gnasheth with his teeth, and pineth away: and I spake to thy disciples that they should cast him out; and they could not. 19 He answereth him, and saith, O faithless generation, how long shall I be with you? how long shall I suffer you? bring him unto me. 20 And they brought him unto him: and when he saw him, straightway the spirit tare him; and he fell on the ground, and wallowed foaming. 21 And he asked his father, How long is it ago since this came unto him? And he said, Of a child. 22 And ofttimes it hath cast him into the fire, and into the waters, to destroy him: but if thou canst do any thing, have compassion on us, and help us. 23 Jesus said unto him, If thou canst believe, all things are possible to him that believeth. 24 And straightway the father of the child cried out, and said with tears, Lord, I believe; help thou mine unbelief. 25 When Jesus saw that the people came running together, he rebuked the foul spirit, saying unto him, Thou dumb and deaf spirit, I charge thee, come out of him, and enter no more into him. 26 And the spirit cried, and rent him sore, and came out of him: and he was as one dead; insomuch that many said, He is dead. 27 But Jesus took him by the hand, and lifted him up; and he arose.

Notice how the father was more than **willing to brag about the demonic afflictions** that were upon his son! Jesus **never asked people what was wrong with them**, but He did ask what they wanted. In most situations, it was obvious what the people needed, but He always asked them what they wanted. *Mark 11:24: "Therefore I say unto you, What things soever ye desire, when ye pray, believe that ye receive them, and ye shall have them."* Jesus always directed people to ask for what they needed: **not to meditate upon the problem**.

On many occasions, when Jesus was surrounded by people who were boasting on the devil, He would direct the needy away from them. We have an example of this in *Matthew 9:18-25*:

While he spake these things unto them, behold, there came a certain ruler, and worshipped him, saying, My daughter is even now dead: but come and lay thy hand upon her, and she shall live. 19 And Jesus arose, and followed him, and so did his disciples....... 23 And when Jesus came into the ruler's house, and saw the minstrels and the people making a noise, 24 He said unto them, Give place: for the maid is not dead, but sleepeth. And they laughed him to scorn. 25 But when the people were put forth, he went in, and took her by the hand, and the maid arose.

Please understand, none of us are walking in **100% faith** all of the time. Sometimes I get out of the will of God. I panic and look at the circumstances and the problem. As I share these truths with you, I am by no means claiming that I have arrived. I am simply coming from a place where I've had many experiences and many wonderful results, by simply following the principles (not a formula) of the Word of God. **We must never boast, never brag, never exalt the devil, and never exalt the circumstance that is contrary to the Word of God.** I can give you a lot of examples, all found in the Bible, of men and women who contradicted God's Word and exalted their problems. Let's just say that it never ended well for them.

Numbers 13 gives a powerful illustration of this when the spies went into the Promised Land that God proclaimed flowed with milk and honey. When the spies returned, they acknowledged what God said was true:

Numbers 13:27 And they told him, and said, We came unto the land whither thou sentest us, and surely it floweth with milk and honey; and this is the fruit of it.

Now, it's wonderful that they acknowledged what God said is true; yet, with their next words they demeaned the promise and called God a liar! They claimed that His promise of protecting and providing for them was false and they exalted their enemies - above God!

Numbers 13:28-9 Nevertheless the people be strong that dwell in the land, and the cities are walled, and very great: and moreover we saw the children of Anak there. 29 The Amalekites dwell in the land of the south: and the Hittites, and the Jebusites, and the Amorites, dwell in the mountains: and the Canaanites dwell by the sea, and by the coast of Jordan.

The information they spewed forth was nothing new. God had already informed them about the enemy, all of their tribal names, and at the same time, He told them that their enemies would be bread for them to eat. Joshua and Caleb spoke up in the midst of their declaration, and declared that God was more than able, if they would simply look to Him, they would be able to overcome. If you read the context of the whole story, you sadly discover that they rose up against these two men of faith, and against God, and Moses - in a violent manner. They said they'd rather have stayed in Egypt, or died in the wilderness, than go back into Canaan to overcome their enemy. God granted their wish and allowed the first generation, out of Egypt, to die in the desert.

I run into believers all the time, Christians, not sinners, that have made devils, demons, problems, sickness and disease in their bodies and minds, much BIGGER THAN GOD!

How can it be that God, who upholds all things with the power of His Word, is not able to overcome the problems of our lives? From Genesis, all the way to the end of the Book of Revelation, God reveals Himself as more than enough: in every situation. Every trial, every affliction and every test simply reveals how big you have made God in your life.

The question we need to ask ourselves is: **How Big Is Our God?** It reminds me of the biblical story of David and Goliath. The Army of Israel were confronted by the Philistines, who had a giant champion soldier, Goliath. For forty days Goliath had challenged any man to face him, but there were none in Israel's army that had enough faith in God to face him. They fled from him.

1 Samuel 17:4 And there went out a champion out of the camp of the Philistines, named Goliath, of Gath, whose height was six cubits and a span......
1 Samuel 10-11 And the Philistine said, I defy the armies of Israel this day; give me a man, that we may fight together. 11 When Saul and all Israel heard those words of the Philistine, they were dismayed, and greatly afraid.
1 Samuel:16 And the Philistine drew near morning and evening, and presented himself forty days.

Along came David, a young shepherd boy; he wonders who this uncircumcised Philistine is that defies the armies of the living God? Now, you have a whole army of men exalting their enemy, Goliath, and you have David saying: "this man is nothing compared to my God." It might sound like David was just full of pride, but in reality, it was faith speaking! Not only did he declare that Goliath was nobody, and nothing, but he was willing to face this giant. I have met many believers who talk a big talk but have little corresponding action.

Faith, when it is in operation, will never exalt, brag, or magnify that which is against the will of God. I hear believers - all the time - exalting their problems, their sicknesses, their afflictions, and their symptoms. When you are truly operating in faith, you will only and always exalt God and His Word. This is an excellent way, I have discovered, to find out **if I'm truly operating in faith.** My mouth gives me away all the time! It reveals (to myself!) where I'm at. There is a tremendous Scripture in the Book of James about this reality:

James 1:22-25 But be ye doers of the word, and not hearers only, deceiving your own selves. 23 For if any be a hearer of the word, and not a doer, he is like unto a man beholding his natural face in a glass: 24 For he beholdeth himself, and goeth his way, and straightway forgetteth what manner of man he was. 25 But whoso looketh into the perfect law of liberty, and continueth therein, he being not a forgetful hearer, but a doer of the work, this man shall be blessed in his deed.

The enemy loves to turn a molehill into a mountain, which we ignorantly and innocently begin to confess over our lives. Now, even if it is truly a mountain: God tells us that we can speak to the mountain and cast it into the sea. Never allow the devil to get you to exalt demonic manifestations, sickness, disease, or afflictions in your body or in others.

Sometimes I think we are a little bit like Israel: a pain in the world's neck. The world absolutely hates the Jews, but can't seem to get rid of them - no matter how they connive, or what they do. God still has a plan and a purpose for their existence. Israel is a sign and a wonder: a divine miracle of the evidence of the reality of God. The world looks at them and says: how in the world can they survive? I believe that the church I pastor is the same. You cannot point to any man-made, natural reasons why we are still in existence. It is all supernatural and divine, as a sign and a wonder, a miracle to show that God is real. While many other churches have shut down, compromised, or just given up … we are still standing strong in Jesus Christ!

#40 I Took Authority Over An Epileptic Seizure At Lowe's (1992)

My wife and I were shopping at a Lowe's building supply store, when all of a sudden, we noticed some commotion at the front of the store. It was at one of the checkout counters. The girl working behind the counter had gone into an epileptic seizure. A small crowd had gathered around the countertop, but nobody was trying to help her. Everybody was standing and staring as she fell to the ground, kicking and squirming. Somebody was calling 9-1-1 to get help. Now, I'm the kind of guy who cannot just be a spectator. So, I walked up and said: "Excuse me," as I pushed my way through all of these people. I said, "Please, let me through, I am a doctor." This was the absolute truth, as I have a Ph.D. in Biblical Theology and a Doctorate of Divinity. I told the people standing there that I could help. I went over to the countertop, having to lean over it to see what was going on. This girl was on the floor thrashing away in a seizure. I simply leaned over the top of the counter, placed one hand on her arm. I whispered real quietly, "In the name of Jesus Christ of Nazareth, you lying devil loose her, and come out of her now!"

Immediately, her eyes stopped rolling; the convulsions stopped, and she got up from off the floor. But, when she stood up, it was not to thank me for helping her. With a demonic snarl, she began to curse and swear at me for taking authority over these demonic spirits. It could have become a brutal battle, but the Spirit quickened me to walk away. This was not the time or place. Plus, the Holy Ghost revealed to me that this girl had invited these demons into her life - to draw attention to her. It saddens my heart over how many people are embracing their infirmities, depressions, and oppressions to use them for their own benefit - either in the form of sympathy or for financial gain.

Timothy 1:7 For God hath not given us the spirit of fear; but of power, and of love, and of a sound mind.

Daniel 11:32 And such as do wickedly against the covenant shall he corrupt by flatteries: but the people that do know their God shall be strong, and do exploits.

Matthew 10:8 Heal the sick, cleanse the lepers, raise the dead, cast out devils: freely ye have received, freely give.

#41 Dog Dying from Distemper Is Healed (2013)

Will God answer prayers when it comes to our animals? The Scriptures declare that He knows every sparrow that falls to the ground. Therefore, He cares about animals. I have a collie dog by the name of Ranger. In the summer of 2013, I was in my office busy with paperwork, when I received a phone call from a lady at the church, Nancy. She was crying and frantic with news that my dog was being attacked by a skunk. I told her I would be right over. By the time I arrived, the skunk was waddling away up the hill, behind the church.

I thought everything was okay because the skunk had been after my dog but they had not come into contact. So, I went back to my office, busy once again with what I needed to get done. As I continued with my work, my phone rang again. When I picked up the phone, it was Nancy again. She was crying and yelling more than before. She said: "Pastor, the skunk is back, and he's in the cage with Ranger! He's attacking Ranger and biting him!"

This time I grabbed my 9mm pistol and ran over to the church, where I had my dog in a kennel. When I arrived, I saw Ranger backed up in the corner of his pen, with this large, very sick, and aggressive skunk going after him. Nancy was standing there crying and calling out for Ranger to come to her. Eventually, I was able to separate my dog from the skunk … and then I sent that skunk to his eternal destiny - wherever that was. Immediately, I knew that this skunk had a real bad case of distemper. His face was all bloated with green pus and his eyes were almost bulging out of his little head.

I pulled out all my dog's veterinary records, and discovered that his distemper shots were not up to date! As I researched it on the internet, I discovered that giving him a distemper shot would not help him, and if he had distemper he would need a miracle. I hoped and prayed that he did not have distemper. A number of days went by when I began to notice that Ranger was not acting normal; he was congested and breathing very hard. He seemed to be listless, and acting strange. The symptoms began to get worse, and worse every day, and his head started to shake, swinging back and forth.

My heart grew heavy because I knew that he had been infected with distemper. I prayed over him half-heartedly, not really having much hope. I finally called up one of the men from church and asked him if he would come down and put my dog out of his misery. He informed me that he would, but he could not do it until the next day.

I was up early the next morning to visit my dog one last time. As I was standing there, it is like the Spirit of God spoke to my heart, and asked me why I was not aggressively believing for my dogs healing. The Holy Spirit was challenging me to trust the Lord, and His Word for my dog to be healed of distemper. As the Spirit of God spoke to my heart, my faith began to rise. I called up the brother that was going to come and put my dog out of his misery, and informed him that I did not need his help; that God was able to turn this situation around.

Once I was off the phone, I grabbed hold of my dog's head, with both hands, and took authority over this demonic attack. I commanded this virus of distemper to let go of Ranger and I informed the enemy that he had no right to trespass on my dog. When I was done speaking to this virus of distemper, I began to praise and worship God and thanked Him that my dog was healed! From then on, I kept on praising the Lord and thanking Him that Ranger would live and not die. All through that day, and for the next two days, I kept praising God - even though it looked like Ranger was getting worse. I just kept on thanking and praising God that it was done, and declaring that the devil is a liar, and that Ranger would live and not die! I declared that the virus had to obey me, in the name of Jesus, and the enemy is defeated! On the third day, I walked out to see Ranger ... Praise the Lord! He was completely normal and back to his old barking, jumping, and tail-wagging self.

That was over two years ago, and he is healthier now than ever! Many times, we give up too soon - instead of aggressively taking a hold of God; we lean on our own understanding. Do not give up! Do not let go! Take a hold of God! Trust Him with whatever situation you are in! God is faithful!

Luke 10:19 Behold, I give unto you power to tread on serpents and scorpions, and over all the power of the enemy: and nothing shall by any means hurt you.

#42 Mountain Man Healed & Restored (2015)

It was the Sunday before Thanksgiving; after the Sunday morning service, Vicki and Linda, two sisters who attend the church I pastor, informed me that their father, William, had suffered a devastating and terrible stroke. The minute they told me, I knew in my heart that I had to get to the hospital to pray for him. I told them that as soon as I could, I would get up to the hospital, that same day.

It was approximately 2 p.m. when I arrived at Chambersburg Hospital, PA. I walked down the hospital hallway, accessed the elevator and pressed the button to the third floor - I was in deep prayer the whole time. There was a great expectation in my heart that God was about to do something wonderful. When I found William in his hospital room the door was hanging slightly open. I entered the room and it was full of family members, who were obviously quite upset. On the bed lay a tall, husky, full white-bearded man. He looked like a mountain man from the old-time books!

The doctor was standing next to the bed giving a report to the family. It was obvious that he was not giving them a good report. The doctor told William's family that he could not guarantee their father would ever recover from this terrible stroke (he was in his seventies) and that he seemed to be in a coma (not that he was) and that he was neither here nor there.

William's eyes were coated with a dull looking white color, and the doctor told his family that their father was blind. He did not know if their father would ever recover his eyesight - even if he recovered from the stroke. Everything the doctor said was negative. There were tears flowing in that hospital room that day. I just stood there quietly, waiting for the doctor to finish, and then to leave. I knew that in the natural, what this doctor was saying was true, but we have access to the One who created all things. I believed in my heart that day that the Great Physician was going to pay them a house call!

Something was stirring in my heart, and I knew what it was. It was the gift of faith that produces immediate results; causing excitement and joy in the hearts of believers. After the doctor left, I walked over to William. He was lying in a state of what looked like death. I spoke up, drawing everybody's attention to me. I told them: "Don't be afraid! Bill is going to be okay." I told them, by the word of wisdom, that his eyesight was going to come back. I told them that his mind was going to be quickened by the spirit of God, and that the Lord was going to raise him up again.

One of the family members asked me: "Are you sure?" I said: "Absolutely! I believe that he will be home for Thanksgiving!" Thanksgiving was only about four days away. Faith rose up in all of the family members that were gathered. Instead of tears of sorrow, now flowed tears of great joy. Some began to cry outright. I said to them: "Now, let's lay hands on William, and take care of this problem." They all gathered around William's bed and started laying their hands on him. I did not pray real loud, but I prayed with authority. In the Name of Jesus I commanded William to be healed, and we all agreed. I commanded for his eyesight, his mind, his reasoning, and his body functions to come back to normal In the Name of Jesus!

When I was done praying, with everybody in total agreement, I said: "Now let us praise God for Bill's complete recovery!" We all began to quietly praise the Lord for answered prayer. The hospital room was now filled with great joy and peace. As I left, I said I was expecting a good report and would be in touch with them; I also encouraged them to have a wonderful Thanksgiving.

Around three days later I was contacted by one of William's daughters. She was extremely excited because her father had made a complete and absolute recovery! His eyesight had come back and his brain and mental awareness had completely returned. That Thanksgiving, he was home eating turkey with the rest of the family. To the writing of this book - he is still doing wonderful. Every day his children walk with him, down the paths and roads of the forest they live in. God still answers prayer when we pray in faith.

CHAPTER TEN

#43 Stabbed In The Face With A Knife By A Demon Possessed Woman! (1977)

Back in 1977, I rode my 750 Honda motorcycle to Oregon to visit a good friend of mine, Judge Lloyd Olds, and his family. I stayed a while in Oregon, and ended up working on a fishing vessel. When it was time to leave Oregon, I rode my motorcycle up the Alcan Freeway, caught a ferry to Alaska, and rode on to Anchorage.

I arrived in Anchorage and the Lord quickened my heart to stop at a small, Full Gospel church that I used to visit. It just so happened that an evangelist I'd known when I was in the Navy (Adak, Alaska) was there too. We spent some time reminiscing about what had happened the previous year, and he shared how the Lord had laid upon his heart to go to Mount Union, Pennsylvania and open up an outreach center. He invited me to go to Pennsylvania, with him and his wife, to open this Evangelistic Outreach Centre. I perceived in my heart that I needed to go with them. So, I made plans to fly back to Wisconsin, where he and his wife would pick me up as they went through. However, before I left Alaska, the Spirit of God had one more assignment for me: a precious woman needed to be set free.

One Sunday we decided to attend a small church along the road to Fairbanks. I was the first to enter this little, old, rustic church. When I went through the sanctuary doors, I immediately noticed a strange, little, elderly, lady across from me - sitting in the pews. She turned her head and stared right at me with the strangest look I have ever seen. I could sense immediately there was something demonic about her. Out of the blue, this little old lady jumped up, got out of the pew, and ran out of the church. At that moment I perceived that God wanted me to go and cast the devils out of her.

When the service was over, I asked the pastor who that elderly lady was. He said she was not a member of his church, but she came once in a great while. He also told me that she lived with her husband in a run-down house on a dirt road. I asked him if it would be okay to go and see her? **(I knew in my heart that God had sent me there to help bring deliverance)** He said he had no problems with this, especially since she wasn't a part of his church.

We followed the directions the pastor gave us, and when we arrived at the house it was exactly as the pastor had described it to us. It was run-down and the yard was overflowing with old furniture and household items. It reminded me of the TV show "Sanford and Son" - but it probably had ten-times more junk in the yard! I do not know how the old couple survived the winters in Alaska in such a poorly-built house. As we got out of the car, a little old man met us outside. It was her husband. He was thanking God as he walked toward us, and said he knew we were men of God, and that we had been sent by the Lord to help his poor, tormented wife. He informed us that his wife was in their kitchen.

So, we walked up to the house, having to go down the twisting and cluttered junk-filled path. We entered the house through a screen door that led into their summer kitchen. When we entered the kitchen, we could see his wife over at a large utility sink. Her back was to us, but we could see she was peeling carrots over her kitchen sink ... with a very large, scary-looking, butchers knife!! As I stood there, looking at the back of her head, I began to speak to her about Jesus. Out of the blue, she turned her head like it was on a swivel to look at me. I could hardly believe my eyes! It was like I was watching a horror movie! This little lady's eyes were glowing red on her swiveled head. I rubbed my eyes at that moment; thinking that maybe I imagined this. No ... her head had swiveled - without her body moving - and her eyes were glowing red. Fear immediately filled my heart as she looked at me with the big knife … a butcher's knife … in her hand. Immediately, I came against the spirit of fear in my heart by quoting the holy Scriptures: **"For God hath not given me the spirit of fear; but of power, and of love, and of a sound mind"** *2 Timothy 1:7.* I shared with her about Jesus Christ. The next thing I knew she was coming right at me - with her knife - as if she was filled with great rage. The knife was still in her right hand when she spun around and came at me. She leapt through the air onto me, wrapping her small skinny legs around my waist. How in the world she was able to do this - I do not know?! The next thing I knew, she was lifting up her right hand and hitting me in the face, very hard, multiple times. I could feel the pressure of her hitting me on the left side of my face. As she was hitting me in the face, out of my mouth came: "In the **Name of Jesus!"**

The minute I came against this attack **"In The Name of Jesus"** she was ripped off of me; picked up by an invisible power, and flung across the room about 10-feet or more. She slammed very hard against the bare wall of her kitchen, and slipped down to the floor. Amazingly when she hit the wall, she was not hurt! I went over to her, continuing to cast the demons out of her In the Name of Jesus. Once I perceived that she was free, and in her right mind, I asked her how she had become demon possessed? She told us her terrible story.

Her uncle had repeatedly molested and raped her when she was a very young girl. She thought she was free from him when he got sick and died. But then he began to visit her from the dead, continuing to molest and rape her at night. To her, it was physical and real. She did not know it was a familiar spirit disguised as her uncle. This had probably gone on for over fifty years! I led her to the Lord. Sweet, beautiful peace came upon her, completely changing her countenance. She was a brand-new person in Christ, finally free - after almost fifty years of torment. She and her husband began to go to church with us - until I left Alaska. I remember that we took them to see the Davis family at a local church, visiting Alaska on a missionary trip.

Years later, the evangelist who visited this lady with me, heard me retelling the story at a church; about how the woman kept punching me forcefully with her right hand. At the end of the service, he came and informed me that I was not telling the story correctly. I wondered if he thought I was exaggerating. He said that he was standing behind me when she jumped on top of me and began to hit me with her right fist.

But, he informed me, it wasn't her hand she was slapping me with ... she still had the large butchers knife in her hand; and he saw her stabbing me in the face with this knife. Repeatedly!! He said he knew that I was a dead man, because nobody could survive being stabbed in the face repeatedly, with a large butcher knife. He expected to see nothing but blood, but instead of seeing my blood everywhere, he saw that there was not even one mark on my face where the knife was hitting me. I did feel something hit my face repeatedly, but I thought it was her hand! Instead, it was her knife, and it could not pierce my skin! Thank God for His love, His mercy, and His Supernatural Divine Protection.

I am convinced that if I had not been walking with God in His holiness and obedience, the devil in that little old lady would have stabbed me to death. Many people in the body of Christ are trying to deal with demonic powers when they are out of the father's will. When we are moving in the Holy Ghost, obedience, and absolute love for Jesus Christ - there is no power in hell that can hurt us!

#43 My Second Son Was Dying From Rabies (2000)

In the year 2000, my son, Daniel, was sixteen-years-old. One day, he brought home a baby raccoon and wanted to keep it as a pet. Immediately, people began to inform me that this was illegal. I further learned, that to have a raccoon in Pennsylvania, you had to purchase one from someone who was licensed by the state to sell them. The reason for this was because of the high rate of rabies carried among them. But stubbornness rose up in my heart against what they were telling me. I hardened my heart and did not listen to my conscience.

You see, I'd had a raccoon when I was a child. The mother had been killed on the highway and left behind a litter of her little-ones. I had taken one of the little-ones home and bottle-fed it. I named her "Candy." I have a lot of fond memories of this raccoon, so when my son wanted to keep his raccoon - against better judgment, against the warnings of my conscience and against the law of the land ... I said okay. I did not realize that baby raccoons could have the rabies virus lying dormant in them for three months before it would manifest. I knew, in my heart, that I was wrong to give Daniel permission to keep this raccoon. But, like so many others, when we are out of the will of God, we justify ourselves. We are completely blind and ignorant of the price that we must pay because of our rebellion and disobedience.

Daniel named his little raccoon "Rascal." And he was a rascal, because he was constantly getting into everything. Several months went by and one night Daniel told me that he'd had a frightening dream. I should have known right then and there that we needed to get rid of this raccoon. He said, in his dream Rascal grew up and became big, like a bear, and then attacked and devoured him. Some time went by and my son began to get sick, running a high fever. One morning, he came downstairs telling me that something was majorly wrong with Rascal. He said that he was wobbling all over the place and was bumping into stuff. Immediately, the alarm bells went off! I asked him where his raccoon was, and he informed me that Rascal was in his bedroom. I ran upstairs to his room, opened his bedroom door, and Rascal was acting extremely strange. He was bumping into everything and had spittle coming from his mouth.

My heart was filled with great dread. I had grown up around wildlife and farm animals: I had run into animals with rabies before. No ifs, ands, or buts ... this raccoon had rabies! I immediately went to Danny and asked him if the raccoon had bitten him, or if he had gotten any of Rascal's saliva in his wounds? He showed me his hands, they were covered in cuts, and he then informed me that he had been letting rascal lick these wounds ... he had even allowed rascal to lick his mouth!

Daniel did not look well and was running a high-grade fever. He also felt dizzy. I knew in my heart that we were in terrible trouble. I immediately called up the local Forest Ranger. They put me on the line with one of their personnel that had a lot of expertise in this area. When I informed him of what was going on, he asked me if I knew it was illegal to take in a wild raccoon. I told him I did know but that I had chosen to ignore the law.

He said that he would come over immediately to our house and examine the raccoon, and if necessary, take it with him. I had placed Rascal in a cage making sure that I did not touch him. When the Forest Ranger arrived, I had the cage sitting in the driveway. He examined the raccoon without touching it. I could tell that he was quite concerned about the condition of this raccoon. He looked at me with deep regret and informed me that, in his opinion, with thirty years wildlife service experience, this raccoon had rabies. He asked me if there was anyone who had been in contact with this raccoon, with any symptoms of sickness. I told him that for the last couple of days, my son Daniel, had not been feeling well. In fact, he was quite sick. When I told him the symptoms Daniel was experiencing, it was obvious the ranger was shaken and quite upset.

He told me that anybody who had been in contact with this raccoon would have to receive shots. He went on to explain that from the description of what Daniel was going through, and considering the length of his illness, it was too late for him! He literally told me that he felt, from his experience, that there was no hope for my son! He fully believed that my son would die from rabies. He loaded the raccoon up in the back of his truck, and left me standing in my driveway weeping. He said that he would get back to me as soon as they had the test results, and that I should get ready for state officials to descend upon myself, my family, and our church.

I cannot express to you the hopelessness and despair that

had struck my heart at that moment. Earlier in the spring our little girl, Naomi, had passed on to be with the Lord, at four-and-a-half years old. And now, my second son, Daniel, was dying from rabies. Both situations could have been prevented.

Immediately, I gathered together my wife; my first son, Michael; my third son, Steven; and my daughter, Stephanie. We all gathered around Daniel's bed and began to **cry out** to God. We wept, cried, and **prayed** - crying out to God. I repented and asked God for mercy. As Daniel was lying on the bed, running a high fever, and almost delirious, he informed me that he was barely able to hang onto consciousness. He said he knew in his heart that he was dying.

After everyone had dispersed from his bed, with great overwhelming sorrow, I went into our family room where we had a wood stove. I opened the wood stove, which still had a lot of cold ashes left from the winter, and I scooped out handful after handful of ashes, pouring it over my head and saturating my body, with tears of repentance and sorrow running down my face. And then I lay in the ashes. The ashes got into my eyes, mouth, and nose and into my lungs, making me quite sick. But I did not care, all that mattered was that God would have mercy on us and spare my son, and all our loved ones, from the rabies virus. As I lay on the floor in the ashes, crying out and praying to God with all I had within me, I could hear the house was filled with weeping, crying, and **praying** family members.

All night long I wept and **prayed**, asking God to please have mercy on my stupidity. To remove the rabies virus not only from my son but from everyone else that had been in contact with this raccoon. I also asked God to remove the virus from Rascal; as a sign that he had heard my prayers. I continued in this state of great agony of **prayer** for over sixteen hours, praying until early in the morning, when suddenly the light of heaven shined upon my soul. Great peace that surpasses all understanding overwhelmed me. I got up with victory in my heart and soul!

I went upstairs to check on Daniel. When I walked into his bedroom, the presence of God was tangible. The fever had broken and he was resting peacefully. Our whole house was filled with the tangible presence of God. From that minute forward, he was completely healed. A couple of days later, I was contacted by the state informing me that, to their amazement, they could find nothing wrong with the raccoon. God had supernaturally removed the rabies virus not only from my son, and those in contact with Rascal, but from the raccoon itself! Thank God that the Lord's mercy endures forever!

Strong FAITH Comes By Delighting In The Word Of God

As we look at this last Chapter on Faith, it will sound like I have already said this, when teaching about abiding in the Word, but, you can abide in the Word without actually delighting yourself in the Word of God.

The Way That Violent Faith Will Come Is By Delighting Yourself In God's Word.

Let me give you an example, you can be married to your mate for fifty years (or longer) and still not really delight yourself in or really enjoy being with your husband or your wife.

Proverbs 5:18 Let thy fountain be blessed: and rejoice with the wife of thy youth.

You can work the same job all of your life, be good at what you do, and yet never really enjoy it. I could give you many illustrations about this, but I think you get my point. We could memorize whole books of the New Testament, thousands of Scriptures, and yet not really delight in them. The definition for the word "delight" means: to rejoice, to take joy, great pleasure, to be happy in, to desire, to be blessed by. A man or woman who delights himself in the law of the Lord, is a person who takes great pleasure and joy in the truth. A person who loves the Word of God.

Psalm 119:16 I will delight myself in thy statutes: I will not forget thy word.

You can even spend hours and days memorizing Scriptures, and meditating upon these truths, and yet not truly love the Word of God. There are many Scriptures in the Old Testament about delighting ourselves not only in God's Word, but in God Himself. But, it will take real faith to develop a love for the truth. In the Book of 2 Thessalonians, Paul warns us by the Spirit of God, that many in the last days will turn away from the truth because they do not love it. And because of their lack of love for God's truth, the Lord will turn them over to a strong spirit of delusion. We see this happening on a massive scale in our generation right now.

2 Thessalonians 2:10-12 And with all deceivableness of unrighteousness in them that perish; because they received not the <u>love of the truth</u>, that they might be saved. 11 And for this cause God shall send them strong delusion, that they should believe a lie: 12 That they all might be damned who believed not the truth, but had pleasure in unrighteousness.

A love for God and His truth must be cultivated within us. This will be a fight of faith because the enemy of our soul wants to devour us through the deceitfulness of this world. Paul The Apostle told us that we can grow by the sincere milk of the Word.

1 Peter 2:2 As newborn babes, desire the sincere milk of the word, that ye may grow thereby:

#44 I BECAME OBSESSED WITH THE DEEP HUNGER OF GOD'S WORD!

I remember giving my heart to **Jesus Christ** on February 18, 1975. As I got up from the floor, born again, saved and delivered, I was a brand-new person. Immediately a **Hunger And Thirst for the Word of God** took a hold of me. I began to devour the Gospels of Matthew, Mark, Luke, and John.

I just could not get enough of the Word of God, because of my love for **Jesus Christ** and His **Father. Jesus** became my hero in every area of my thoughts and daily life. He became my reason for getting up, going to work, eating, sleeping, and living. I discovered that everything I did was based on the desire of wanting to please Him. I carried my little green military Bible with me wherever I went. Whenever I had an opportunity I would open it up and study it. It wasn't very long before I believed for a larger Bible. This larger Bible gave me much more room to make notes, highlight and circle certain Scriptures. The more I fed on the Scriptures: the greater my hunger became for them.

I probably wasn't even saved for two months before I was asked to speak, for the first time, at a small Pentecostal church. I believe it was called "Adak Full Gospel Church." As far as I know, it was the only Pentecostal church on the military base situated on an Aleutian Island, in Alaska. Since 1975 I have never lost my hunger, or my thirst for God's Word. I can even truly say what the psalmist said:

Psalm 104:34 My meditation of him shall be sweet: I will be glad in the Lord.

The hunger for God's Word has caused me to memorize over one-third of the New Testament. I am not bragging or boasting, I'm just simply saying that God's Word is the joy and rejoicing of my heart. There are People Who Love to Swim, People Who Love to Work out, People Who Love to Do Push-Ups and Chin-Ups and Lift Weights - but we need people who love God's Word!

Psalm 16:3 But to the saints that are in the earth, and to the excellent, in whom is all my delight.

Psalm 37:4 Delight thyself also in the LORD: and he shall give thee the desires of thine heart.

Psalm 37:23 The steps of a good man are ordered by the LORD: and he delighteth in his way.

Psalm 40:8 I delight to do thy will, O my God: yea, thy law is within my heart.

Psalm 112:1 Praise ye the LORD. Blessed is the man that feareth the LORD, that delighteth greatly in his commandments.

Psalm 119:16 I will delight myself in thy statutes: I will not forget thy word.

Psalm 119:24 Thy testimonies also are my delight and my counselors.

Psalm 119:35 Make me to go in the path of thy commandments; for therein do I delight.

Psalm 119:47 And I will delight myself in thy commandments, which I have loved.

Psalm 119:70 ......but I delight in thy law.

Psalm 119:77 Let thy tender mercies come unto me, that I may live: for thy law is my delight.

Psalm 119:92 Unless thy law had been my delights, I should then have perished in mine affliction.

Psalm 119:143 Trouble and anguish have taken hold on me: yet thy commandments are my delights.

Psalm 119:174 I have longed for thy salvation, O LORD; and thy law is my delight.

Psalm 104:34 My meditation of him shall be sweet: I will be glad in the LORD.

We have now reached the conclusion on this particular subject. Yet, I'm sure that there is a tremendous amount more we could say about "**The Violent Take It By Force.**" I hope and pray that you begin to apply each one of the Spiritual Principles and Truths. The greatest need we have in this generation are those who truly have Faith, Confidence, Reliance, Dependence and Trust In God. Jesus boldly declared that all things are possible to those who believe in Him! May this generation rise up in the Power and the Faith of Jesus Christ, going forth and setting the captives free.

Sincerely: Dr Michael H Yeager

How To Live In The Miraculous!

This is a quick explanation of how to live and move in the realm of the miraculous. Seeing divine interventions of God is not something that just spontaneously happens because you have been born-again. There are certain biblical principles and truths that must be evident in your life. This is a very basic list of some of these truths and laws:

1. You must give Jesus Christ your whole heart. You cannot be lackadaisical in this endeavour. Being lukewarm in your walk with God is repulsive to the Lord. He wants 100% commitment. Jesus gave His all! Now it is our turn to give our all. He loved us 100%. Now we must love Him 100%.

Proverbs 23:26 My son, give me thine heart, and let thine eyes observe my ways
Revelation 3:16 So then because thou art lukewarm, and neither cold nor hot, I will spew thee out of my mouth.

2. There must be a complete agreement with God's Word. We must be in harmony with the Lord; in our attitude, actions, thoughts, and deeds. Whatever the Word of God declares in the New Testament is what we wholeheartedly agree with.

Amos 3:3 Can two walk together, except they be agreed?

2 Chronicles 16:9 For the eyes of the LORD run to and fro throughout the whole earth, to shew himself strong in the behalf of them whose heart is perfect toward him ...

3. Obey and do the Word of God from the heart: from the simplest to the most complicated request or command. No matter what the Word says to do - Do it! Here are some simple examples: Lift your hands in praise, in everything give thanks, forgive instantly, gather together with the saints, and give offerings to the Lord, and so on.

John 5:30 I can of mine own self do nothing: as I hear, I judge: and my judgment is just; because I seek not mine own will, but the will of the Father which hath sent me.

4. Make Jesus the highest priority of your life. Everything you do, do not do it as unto men, but do it as unto God.

Colossians 3:1-2 If ye then be risen with Christ, seek those things which are above, where Christ sitteth on the right hand of God. 2 Set your affection on things above, not on things on the earth.

5. Die to self! The old man says: "My will be done!" The new man says: "God's will be done!"

Galatians 2:20 I am crucified with Christ: nevertheless I live; yet not I, but Christ liveth in me: and the life which I now live in the flesh I live by the faith of the Son of God, who loved me, and gave himself for me.

Romans 6:8 Now if we be dead with Christ, we believe that we shall also live with him:

6. Repent the minute you get out of God's will—no matter how minor, or small the sin may seem.

Revelation 3:19 As many as I love, I rebuke and chasten: be zealous therefore, and repent.

7. Take one step at a time. God will test you (not to do evil) to see if you will obey Him. *Whatever He tells you to do: by His Word, by His Spirit, or within your conscience ... Do it!* He will never tell you to do something contrary to His nature or His Word!

Matthew 12:50 For whosoever shall do the will of my Father which is in heaven, the same is my brother, and sister, and mother.

2 Kings 5:14 Then went he down, and dipped himself seven times in Jordan, according to the saying of the man of God: and his flesh came again like unto the flesh of a little child, and he was clean.

ABOUT THE AUTHOR

Dr. Michael and Kathleen Yeager have served as pastors/apostles, missionaries, evangelists, broadcasters and authors for over four decades. They flow in the gifts of the Holy Spirit, teaching the Word of God with wonderful signs and miracles following in confirmation of God's Word. In 1983, they began Jesus is Lord Ministries International, Biglerville, PA 17307.

Websites Connected to Doc Yeager

www.docyeager.com

www.jilmi.org

www.wbntv.org

Some of the Books Written by Doc Yeager:

"Living in the Realm of the Miraculous #1"

"I Need God Cause I'm Stupid"

"The Miracles of Smith Wigglesworth"

"How Faith Comes 28 WAYS"

"Horrors of Hell, Splendors of Heaven"

"The Coming Great Awakening"

"Sinners In The Hands of an Angry GOD", (modernized)

"Brain Parasite Epidemic"

"My JOURNEY To HELL" - illustrated for teenagers

"Divine Revelation Of Jesus Christ"

"My Daily Meditations"

"Holy Bible of JESUS CHRIST"

"War In The Heavenlies - (Chronicles of Micah)"

"Living in the Realm of the Miraculous #2"

"My Legal Rights To Witness"

"Why We (MUST) Gather!- 30 Biblical Reasons"

"My Incredible, Supernatural, Divine Experiences"

"Living in the Realm of the Miraculous #3"

"How GOD Leads & Guides! - 20 Ways"

"Weapons Of Our Warfare"

"How You Can Be Healed"

"God Still Heals"

Made in the USA
Coppell, TX
26 December 2021